Lucid, vigorous and brief

Advice to new writers

Lucid, vigorous and brief

Advice to new writers

PETER FRYER

Index Books
London

© Peter Fryer 1998

First published 1993
Second edition, revised and expanded, published 1998

Published by Index Books
10-12 Atlantic Road, Brixton, London SW9 8HY

Typeset by Sumner Type, London SE22

Printed by Trade Union Printing Services, Newcastle upon Tyne

A C.I.P. catalogue record for this book is available
from the British Library

ISBN 1-871518-23-7

CONTENTS

INTRODUCTION

This booklet is a revised and expanded version of articles that appeared at intervals in the weekly *Workers Press* in 1991–92. In revising it I have tried to make of it the sort of booklet I myself would have found helpful when I became a junior reporter on leaving school at the age of sixteen.

I agree with the Fowler brothers, authors of *The King's English* (1906), that anyone who wants to write well should try to be 'direct, simple, brief, vigorous, and lucid'. Of those desirable qualities, I count lucidity the most desirable of all. So I have tried to make this booklet as clear as possible and shall welcome criticism of any lack of clarity, or any other shortcoming, that may be found in it. Writers who presume to advise others how to write can't legitimately complain if their own writing is put under the microscope. And among the many examples of how not to write that I have provided here, with suggested corrections, is one caused by my own carelessness and failure to read critically what I had written.

The first thing the would-be writer has to learn—and how I wish somebody had told me this 50 years ago—is the difference between amateurism and professionalism. Amateurs write only when they feel like it; professionals write whether they feel like it or not. If you're serious about writing you will chain yourself to your desk with the most rigorous of invisible chains. You will give writing top priority in your life and organise your time accordingly. And even if you have no ambition to be a professional writer but simply want to make occasional acceptable contributions to newspapers or magazines, you should do your best to bring those contributions up to the highest possible standard. That means taking a professional attitude; above all, it means hard work.

I don't mean that you'll never relax. Even Samuel Johnson, for whom dictionary-making was drudgery—a lexicographer was 'a harmless drudge', but a drudge all the same—could be persuaded to lay down his pen and go to the pub on occasion. There's a story about some cronies arriving late at night to take him out for a drink, and the 'Doctor' calling from his window: 'Very well, you dogs, I'll have a frolic with you.' But with Johnson, as with every serious writer, his work came first and his frolics second. He really cherished the drudgery that was an inescapable part of his work. And that is surely the acid test of professionalism.

Whether you aim to write full- or part-time, you have to find out for yourself the conditions under which you work best and be ruthless in establishing those conditions, in defending your working space and working time. Some people write best in a library; others are more comfortable at home. Find out which you prefer and stick to it. Establish regular working habits and don't let anyone or anything divert you from them or otherwise distract you.

In this new edition I have made a few minor revisions, incorporated some fresh examples of bad or mediocre writing, and added a chapter answering some of the questions that readers of the first edition have asked. I am grateful to Bridget Leach and Norma Meacock for much helpful criticism and advice, and to Orlanda Ward for defending the first edition of this booklet, with a courage beyond her years, against her English teacher's strictures.

P.F.

1 July 1998

1

THE TOOLS OF YOUR TRADE

Though writing can be an art, it is first of all a craft. And its mastery, like that of any other craft, entails the mastery of certain tools. Just as carpenters and bricklayers have to know the tools of their trade, and know them thoroughly, so writers have to acquire certain tools and learn how to use them to best advantage.

This obviously means, first of all, a pencil and paper, though nowadays the serious writer will graduate as soon as possible to a word processor. But there are other tools, hardly less vital, in the shape of the reference books that you should have at your elbow as you write, or at any rate within easy reach, so that you have no excuse to leave your desk.

For a start, you should buy the best dictionary you can afford. I recommend *The Shorter Oxford English Dictionary*, which gives a potted history of every word in the language as well as quotations showing the contexts in which various writers have used particular words in the past. Its main drawback is its cost; until you've managed to save up for it, both *The Concise Oxford Dictionary* and *Collins Concise Dictionary* are useful substitutes. There will be times when you feel the need to turn to the multi-volume *Oxford English Dictionary*, properly titled *A New English Dictionary on Historical Principles*, though no one ever calls it that; most people say *OED*. Few individuals can afford to buy this great work, but there are sets in many local libraries. For the preferred spelling where there is a choice, and for sensible rulings on capitalisation, hyphens, italics, and other matters of style, *The Oxford Writers' Dictionary*, compiled by R.E. Allen, is invaluable. A good dictionary, by the way, has far more to offer than mere guidance on spelling. Used intelligently, it can often help you find the best words and may even suggest how they can be put together to best effect.

H.W. Fowler's *Modern English Usage*, first published in 1926 and recently revised, deserves a place on every writer's reference shelf. Much of the advice contained in Wilson Follett's lesser-known *Modern American Usage* applies, despite its title, to writers of English on this side of the Atlantic too. And, at the suggestion of my friend Simon Pirani, I gladly add to these recommendations a book I hadn't read six years ago when I wrote the articles on which the present booklet is based: Keith Waterhouse's *Waterhouse on Newspaper Style* (1989). I can't imagine any aspirant writer not learning a lot, as I have done, from this plain-spoken champion of plain English against its enemies: clichés, officialese, tabloidese, and many others.

The Oxford Dictionary of Quotations and *The Penguin Dictionary of Quotations* are both worth having to hand. *The Oxford Companion to English Literature* is a mine of information on matters far wider than its title suggests. A good world atlas with a substantial gazetteer is a wise investment and, if you're writing on any aspect of British history, so are a historical atlas and the two-volume *Concise Dictionary of National Biography*. The best single-volume reference work on current affairs is the annual *Whitaker's Almanack*.

One reference book the beginner should be warned about is Roget's *Thesaurus of English Words and Phrases*. Peter Mark Roget, a physician who became a professor of physiology and invented a new kind of slide-rule, published this well-known book in 1852. That was still, in the natural sciences, the great age of classification and Roget was consciously influenced by the eighteenth-century Swedish naturalist Linnaeus, who had laid the basis for the modern classification of plants and animals. Roget wrote in the Introduction to his *Thesaurus*:

> The principle by which I have been guided in framing my verbal classification is the same as that which is employed in the various

departments of natural history. Thus the sectional divisions I have formed correspond to natural families in botany and zoology, and the filiation [i.e. genealogical relationship] of words presents a network analogous to the natural filiation of plants or animals.

There are six main divisions—Abstract Relations, Space, Matter, Intellect, Volition, and Affections—and, within those, innumerable sub- and sub-sub-divisions. Terms with opposite meanings are arranged in adjacent columns, and a bulky index enables the inquirer to find whole lists of synonyms and antonyms. Unfortunately these lists are not annotated in any way. Formal and colloquial expressions, slang and old-fashioned turns of phrase are mixed up together in—to give one example—a 'farrago, jumble, mess, salad, sauce, hash, hodge-podge or hotch-potch, mash, mish-mash, job lot, omnium gatherum, gallimaufry, olla podrida, olio, salmagundi, pot-pourri, Noah's ark, cauldron, marquetry, mosaic, complex'. According to Roget no guidance is needed, since 'an instinctive tact will rarely fail to lead [the user] to the proper choice' of word.

Yet it is just this 'instinctive tact' which is undeveloped in the beginner. Only by wide reading can a writer develop a large and precise vocabulary and gain some understanding of the subtle distinctions among the synonyms and near-synonyms in which the English language is so rich. Experienced writers may spend a long time choosing a word, perhaps a strange or exotic one, to express their exact shade of meaning, and in the hands of such writers 'Roget' has its uses. In a beginner's hands it can be a recipe for disaster, encouraging floweriness, pretentiousness, and a piling up of adjectives. Learning how to write from Roget's classified word-lists is like learning how to make a garden from a seed catalogue.

2

WORKING WITH WORDS

Words are the writer's building-blocks. Just as a person constructing a drystone wall has to select stones of appropriate weight, size and shape, and fit them together properly, so the writer's first task is to select the appropriate words and fit them together properly. The writer's quarry, as it were, is the entire English vocabulary, that rich and constantly growing store of words which often have overlapping or identical meanings, so that there is usually a problem of choice.

Choice is made easier if we remember that the English vocabulary can be classified according to usage and currency.

At the centre of the quarry is a huge stock of words common to literature and everyday speech. At either side of this central pile are two other piles: one of literary words, the other of colloquial words. The literary words are English in its Sunday best. Formal or dignified at best, pompous at worst, these are words not generally used in everyday speech; but in the written language they can sometimes be very effective, so long as they're not over-used. The colloquial words are English with its jacket off and its sleeves rolled up. Some people think these workaday words are too informal for serious writing; but again, so long as they're not over-used, they can be very effective.

Then, separate but not fenced off from these three main piles of words, there are several smaller piles. There are archaic or old-fashioned words; local or dialect words; technical and scientific terms; slang words; 'vulgarisms' (i.e. colloquialisms that the present generation of dictionary-makers think are 'low' or 'unrefined', though their successors may well not agree with them); and foreign words that have not yet become naturalised. I said 'not fenced off' because there is a constant flow of words among these different categories. Yesterday's literary word may tomorrow rank as an archaism; many of the day before yesterday's slang words (e.g. 'mob') have become quite acceptable even in written English; the not-yet-naturalised foreign word often sheds its exotic flavour and may do so quite quickly.

Writers who want to be as clear as possible, to be understood by the widest possible audience, are well advised to choose as far as they can from the first pile I mentioned: that central stock of words common to literature and everyday speech. The first rule, then, is to call a spade a spade. If you find yourself calling it a horticultural implement you've chosen an expression from the literary pile and ought to ask yourself whether 'spade' wouldn't work better. If you find yourself calling it a bloody shovel you've chosen an expression from the colloquial pile—older and more conventional people might even brand this expression a vulgarism—and should consider whether it expresses the exact shade of meaning you wish to convey. It may be that a literary word or a colloquialism does express your meaning precisely. If so, go ahead. For writing that totally avoids literary words runs the danger of getting a bit slack and sloppy, just as writing that totally avoids colloquialisms can lack colour and vigour.

The important thing is to be aware of these distinctions. Good writing doesn't mean just slapping down the first thing that comes into your head and then giving it a cursory rereading. You have to know what you're doing; you have to know which pile a particular word comes from. This is especially important if you choose an archaism, a dialect word, a technical or scientific term, a slang word, a colloquialism, or a foreign expression. All of these have their place. Obliging a writer to avoid them altogether is—to change the metaphor from the quarry to the kitchen—like forbidding a cook to use salt or pepper. But they should be the exception, not the rule. And usually it's better to explain them.

Political writing in particular, when it seeks precision, cannot always avoid technical and scientific terms. 'Dictatorship of the proletariat', 'political revolution', 'permanent revolution', 'cadre', and so on: all have their place in such writing. But it should be borne in mind that 99 people out of 100 don't understand these expressions. To the man and woman on the Clapham omnibus 'dictatorship' calls to mind Hitler and 'permanent' means going on for ever. So, if we want what we write to be generally understood rather than intelligible to merely a small circle of initiates, we must explain the technical and scientific terms we use.

But let's take an example from an entirely different field. Here's a passage that appeared some years ago in the *Guardian* obituary of the Indian musician Mallikarjun Mansur:

> He often dispensed with *druta* (fast) elaboration of a *khayaal* (a north Indian classical style) in favour of a more leisurely, *vilambit* unfolding of a *raaga*.
>
> His *aalaap* (introductory exposition of the *raaga)* was merged into *barhata* (unfolding of *raaga* accompanied by rhythm patterns). He was a master of subtle ornamentation: his intricate *taana* (rapid sequence of equal duration and *vaakra taans* (zigzag *taans* or *fioriture* in Western musical language) were legendary. (Jyotirmaya Sharma)

A bracket is obviously missing after 'duration', but even with that correction such a mass of inadequately explained technical terms is intolerable because unintelligible. The writer has taken on an impossible task; if the space allowed him was limited, as no doubt it was, he should have confined himself to a lucid description of the musician's style in general terms instead of getting bogged down in technical details.

Abbreviations of names of trades unions and other organisations count as technical terms. However familiar any abbreviation may be to you, do remember that to many of your readers it won't be nearly so familiar. So explain each abbreviation the first time you use it, and above all avoid strings of abbreviations.

Choosing the right word is a job of work. It means being sensitive in two directions: to your language and its immense resources and variety; to your readers and their level of understanding.

The first sort of sensitivity—to the language—is best gained not by consulting grammars of English or even books on how to write but, as I said in the previous chapter, by reading widely. Reading a variety of books, including the classics of English literature, is the most reliable road both to an enhanced vocabulary and to a sure grasp of how to deploy it.

The second sort of sensitivity—to your audience—is best acquired by having some particular person in mind as you write: a relative or friend. Write as if you were writing them a letter. Always remember that writing is communicating. Effective writing means getting ideas out of one mind into another. Obscurity, jargon, unexplained technicalities, a profusion of literary words: these are barriers to communication. On the other hand, patronising your readers by deliberately writing down to them is also a barrier to communication, and an offensive one.

If you write for your own amusement or to show how clever you are and what out-of-the-way words you know, you'll soon lose most of your readers, and you'll deserve to. Equally, if you treat your readers like small children who can't be expected to understand words of more than one syllable, or to follow an argument of any complexity, then you risk the same reaction.

So an intelligent approach to the problem of choosing the best word—a problem that confronts you as soon as you put pen to paper or sit down at the word processor—is your first essential step on the road to becoming an effective writer. Here are some practical rules to help you in your choice. They were drawn up by H.W. Fowler and F.G. Fowler as long ago as 1906 and they still hold good today, as do some of the examples they gave and some of those that H.W. Fowler gave later in *Modern English Usage*. I have borrowed freely from both but have taken some examples from elsewhere and have added some of my own.

1. Prefer the familiar word or expression to the far-fetched, and the concrete to the abstract.

'Continual vigilance is imperative.' Here is a patch of verbal fog through which a thought is hazily looming. So blow the fog away and express the identical thought more clearly and simply: 'We must be on the watch.'

'No year passes now without evidence of the truth of the statement that . . . ' Foggy and cumbersome. Put the same thought in plain, down-to-earth English: 'Every year shows again how true it is that . . .'

'Participation by the workers in the control of the industry is non-existent.' Weak and woolly. Suggested rewrite: 'The workers have no part in the control of the industry.'

'The availability of this material is diminishing.' What's wrong with 'This material is becoming scarcer'?

'Was this the realisation of an anticipated liability?' This means 'Did you expect you would have to do this?' So why not put it like that?

This kind of writing, so beloved of half-educated officials and politicians, is a disease. There's a name for this disease: 'abstractitis'. Writers who suffer from it automatically and unthinkingly put an abstract word in command as the subject of the sentence, thus shoving into the background people and what they do, things and what is done to them.

Sir Arthur Quiller-Couch, in his 1913–14 Cambridge lectures *On the Art of Writing*, quoted Don Quixote's squire, Sancho Panza: 'How excellent a thing is sleep; it wraps a man round like a cloak.' Then he 'translated' this as a writer suffering from 'abstractitis' might put it: 'Among the beneficent qualities of sleep its capacity for withdrawing the human consciousness from the contemplation of immediate circumstances may perhaps be accounted not the least remarkable.' You can see at a glance which is better. Similarly 'the absence of intelligence is an indication of satisfactory developments' is a ham-fisted way of saying 'no news is good news'. And Marx and Engels, beginning their *Communist Manifesto*, didn't write: 'The deepening class contradictions manifesting themselves on the

European continent in the present conjuncture are reflected in the disturbing apparition of a politico-philosophical phenomenon seeking revolutionary hegemony.' What they did write was concrete, arresting, memorable, simple, and clear: 'A spectre is haunting Europe—the spectre of communism.'

So remember: abstract nouns muffle your thoughts like cotton wool. The fewer of them you allow into your writing, the clearer it will be.

2. Prefer the single word to the roundabout expression.

The word 'case' is the lazy writer's favourite stand-by. It is the enemy of clarity and brevity. Nine times out of ten it blurs any sentence in which it is used, as the following examples show:

'Inaccuracies were in many cases due to cramped methods of writing.' 'In many cases' simply means 'often'. Why use three words where one will do?

'. . . a few examples of remarkably fine penmanship in the case both of boys and girls.' The last eight words here can with advantage be cut to four: '. . . by both boys and girls.'

'In many cases the answers lacked care.' Seven words where four will do much better: 'Many answers lacked care.'

'In the first two volumes, the chapter "Onomastics" is in each case written by Cecily Clark' (Randolph Quirk). Suggested rewrite: 'In each of the first two volumes the chapter "Onomastics" is written by', etc.

'In many cases, the dogs, unclear why their lives had been so dislocated, attacked the intruders, inflicting serious wounds' (Patrick Cockburn). This sentence sprouts two growths of fur: 'in many cases' and 'inflicting'. So let's trim these off. Suggested rewrite: 'Many of the dogs, unclear why their lives had been so dislocated, attacked the intruders and seriously wounded them.'

'I have also enjoyed the Australian Les Murray's new volume *Subhuman Redneck Poems* (Carcanet) and Ian Hamilton's poem sequence Steps (Cargo). Unexpectedly, the two have something in common: an uncontemporary feel for traditional cadence and metre, which in both cases remind me of Philip Larkin' (John Bayley).

Better would be 'in both books' or 'in both poets' (and 'remind', since the antecedent of 'which' is the singular noun 'feel', should be corrected to 'reminds').

'The fact that, in the case of this reader, his struggle only partly succeeded is surely—I am left feeling—my fault, not his' (Richard Dawkins). Better would be 'for this reader'; better still, 'The fact that this reader's struggle', etc.

'The number of books, articles, films, and television programs devoted to them [i.e. Hitler's life and career] is greater than in the case of any of the other national leaders of the century.' (Gordon A. Craig). Suggested rewrite: 'More books, articles, films, and television programs have been devoted to Hitler's life and career than to those of any other national leader of this century.'

'There really were cases of gangsters firing revolvers at one another across the theatre, in at least one case with fatal results' (Richard Boston). Suggested rewrite: 'Gangsters really did sometimes fire revolvers at each other across the theatre, at least once with fatal results.'

'Basis', however common it is in the spoken language, is another word the writer should use with the utmost caution. There is no excuse for 'on a daily basis', 'on a weekly basis', and suchlike phrases with which lazy or hasty writers befog their prose. 'For those of us . . . who don't have to work with it on a daily basis, quantum mechanics can be pretty off-putting' (John Durant). 'In reality, he is subjected to such indignities for the Duchess's amusement on a daily basis' (Lavinia Greenlaw). 'It is this sector of the drug economy, and the plight of those who live and work in it on a day-to-day basis, which deserves attention' (Vincenzo Ruggiero). In all three of these quotations, 'every day' or 'each day' would be preferable—and, in the last one, the subject being plural ('sector . . . and plight'), 'deserves' should be corrected to 'deserve'; cf. pp. 48-9 below.

Similarly with 'level', another lazy choice: 'The current talks have been mainly on the technical level.' More fur. Rewrite thus: 'The current talks have been mainly technical.' 'Sales reductions at the retail level have led to pessimism.' What's wrong with 'Reductions in retail sales'? 'Many problems can be avoided if they are anticipated at the manufacturing level.' Rewrite: '. . . anticipated by the manufacturers.'

In short, whenever you find yourself writing 'in the case of' or 'on a — basis', 'at the — level', 'of a — character', or 'of a — nature', a warning bell should ring in your head and you should consider replacing the circumlocution with a single word. Similarly, 'in short supply' can generally be replaced by 'scarce', and 'was made the recipient of' by 'was presented with'.

Is an 'end result' different from a mere 'result'? Since a gift is by definition free, why call it a 'free gift'? Since a haven is by definition safe, what is gained by calling it a 'safe haven'? No one has yet found a way to plan the past, so 'forward planning' is a silly substitute for 'planning'. 'Weather conditions' is never an improvement on 'weather'; nor 'height levels' on 'heights'; nor 'behaviour patterns' on 'behaviour'.

3. Prefer the short word to the long.
Do you envisage an eventuality or face an event? Are adverse climatic conditions any different from bad weather? Is answering in the affirmative anything more than saying yes? Police officers might tell the magistrates that they proceeded on foot to such-and-such a place; the rest of us walked there. 'He was conveyed to his place of residence in an intoxicated condition' is a pompous way of writing 'He was carried home drunk.'

Sometimes, of course, there's no satisfactory alternative to a long word. For instance, there's no short word for 'circumlocution', which I used several paragraphs above.

4. In general, prefer a word of Germanic origin (a 'Saxon' word) to one derived from a Romance language (i.e. a language descended from Latin).
Examples: 'Despite the unfavourable climatic conditions' should be replaced by 'Bad as the weather has been'; 'He expired in indigent circumstances', by 'He died poor'.

An 'educated' young person was explaining something to her

grandmother. 'Take an egg', she said, 'and make a perforation in the base and a corresponding one in the apex. Then apply the lips to the aperture, and by forcibly inhaling the breath the shell is entirely discharged of its contents.'

'Goodness me!' exclaimed the old woman. 'When I was a girl they made a hole in each end and sucked.'

These four practical rules, which obviously overlap, should be taken as guidelines only, not as rigid rules that must never be broken on any account. But beginners should be aware of them and keep them always in mind. It's a good idea to put away every completed piece of writing for a few hours—better still, for a few days or weeks: for as long as possible, in fact—and then reread it as if someone else had written it, checking whether these rules have been kept. Such rereading and, where necessary, revision are an essential part of the writer's work.

Careful revision is a sort of quality control. It's a sign of skill, professionalism, and pride in your work.

3

HOW TO WRITE A SENTENCE

We have been looking at how to select the appropriate words. Now we are going to look at how to fit them together properly in a sentence.

There are countless definitions of a sentence. Some say it's a group of words that makes sense; others, that it's a complete thought. A more pragmatic and probably more useful definition is that it's the words which come between two full stops. This popular definition will do pretty well, if we take full stop to include question mark and exclamation mark, and if we remember that a sentence can break off with a dash, as often happens in dialogue. Some pundits insist that a sentence has to have a verb in it, but this is a requirement that matters to grammarians, not to writers. 'So far so good.' 'Of course not.' 'True, no doubt.' 'Yes.' 'No.' 'Perhaps.' Whatever the grammarian may say, to the writer these are all sentences, though none has a verb.

Roughly speaking, the average length of the sentences in a piece of writing ought not to exceed 25 words, and seldom should any sentence run to more than 50 words. If the average sentence length exceeds 25 words many readers will find that piece of writing hard going. An occasional long sentence is no bad thing, provided the writer keeps a grip on it and organises it properly. But a succession of long sentences soon grows tedious. And writers who lose their grip in a long sentence thereby lose their readers. Here's an example from a *Guardian* book review:

Preparation for a recent trip I made to Egypt began very seriously, with the American mystery-writer and archaeologist Elizabeth Peters (author of *Crocodile On The Sandbank*, until very recently OP) whose 19th century sleuth, Amelia Peabody, is based on the intrepid Amelia Edwards, the Victorian writer who explored ancient Egypt in the 1870s, when with five friends she hired the 'Philae', a *dahabeeyah* capacious enough to carry six passengers in great comfort, and a crew of 20, who seem to have stowed themselves away as best they could in available nooks and crannies. (Margaret Riches)

This meandering sentence of 94 words might have been mended by turning the comma after 'Edwards' into a full stop and starting a new sentence thus: 'This Victorian writer explored . . . ' But there are many other possible ways of improving it and, as an exercise, you might try doing so yourself.

The reader should now take a very deep breath and then read aloud these two consecutive sentences from an article in *The New York Review of Books*, the first running to 101 words, the second to 121:

D'Souza's intention in *Ronald Reagan: How an Ordinary Man Became an Extraordinary Leader*, which, like his 1991 *Illiberal Education: The Politics of Race and Sex on Campus* and his 1995 *The End of Racism: Principles for a Multiracial Society*, was written within the nurturing grant framework of the American Enterprise Institute, was to offer what he presents as a 'revisionist' view of the Reagan years, a correction of the record for 'a new generation of young people' who, because they have had 'no alternative source of information', have been unable to detect the 'transparent bias' of their teachers and the media.

It is D'Souza's thesis, honed by his useful and apparently inexhaustible ability to present himself as one of a besieged minority, that Reagan has been systematically misread, not only by his 'liberal critics' (further identified as 'the pundits, political scientists, and historians', 'the wise men', 'the intellectual elite', and 'the cognoscenti') and not only by his own more pragmatic aides (the 'prags', or 'ingrates and apostates'), whose remarkably similar descriptions of the detachment at the center of the administration in which they served seem to D'Souza to be 'characterized by an almost defiant disloyalty', but even by his 'hard-core' admirers, or 'true believers', those movement conservatives who considered the President a 'malleable figurehead' too often controlled by his pragmatist advisers. (Joan Didion)

These are truly dreadful sentences, all the more appalling since they were penned by one of the USA's most distinguished novelists and approved by the editors of that country's most distinguished intellectual journal. How should these top-heavy sentences have been lightened? Here is one way:

Like two of D'Souza's earlier books [their titles and dates can be given in a footnote], *Ronald Reagan* [its full title appears at the head of the article and therefore need not be repeated] was written within the nurturing grant framework of the American Enterprise Foundation. In this book D'Souza intended to offer what he presents as a 'revisionist' view of the Reagan years. He aimed to correct the record for 'a new generation of young people' who, because they have had 'no alternative source of information', have been unable to detect the 'transparent bias' of their teachers and the media.

D'Souza presents himself as one of a besieged minority. His ability to do so, which is both useful and apparently inexhaustible, hones his thesis that Reagan has been systematically misread. And it is not only Reagan's 'liberal critics'—further identified as 'the pundits, political scientists, and historians', 'the wise men', 'the intellectual elite', and 'the cognoscenti'—who have misread him. So have his own more pragmatic aides—the 'prags' or 'ingrates and apostates'—whose remarkably similar descriptions of the detachment at the center of the administration they served in seem to D'Souza to be 'characterized by an almost defiant disloyalty'. Reagan has been misread even by his 'hard-core' admirers or 'true believers', those movement conservatives who considered the President a 'malleable figurehead' too often controlled by his pragmatist advisers.

One final example of an overlong sentence in which the writer has lost his grip, this time from a book review in the *Observer:*

> In his fine (and here much-quoted) autobiography he says 'My boyhood
> was, I think, as unhappy as that of a young gentleman could well be',
> partly due to his father's hopeless mismanagement of his affairs and
> partly because his own physical ugliness and clumsy-wittedness created
> what he memorably called an 'utter want . . . of that juvenile manhood
> which enables some boys to hold up their heads'. (Andrew Motion)

This 65-word sentence would be greatly improved by being split
into two. There should be a full stop after 'could well be'. Then, in
the second sentence, a careful writer would avoid changing horses
in mid-stream ('partly due' followed by 'partly because'), would
choose a verb in place of the noun 'mismanagement', and would
therefore write 'He was unhappy partly because his father hope-
lessly mismanaged his affairs, partly because his own physical
ugliness', etc.

Just as the rule of thumb about sentences averaging no more than
25 words doesn't mean that no sentence may be long, nor does it
mean that every sentence must be short. Or very short. Like this. A
succession of very short sentences is jerky and soon gets on readers'
nerves, just as an unbroken sequence of very long ones soon tires
them out. If you vary the length of your sentences you have a far
better chance of holding your readers' attention.

You will more easily hold their attention, too, if you vary the
structure of your sentences, i.e. the way in which they are made up
of clauses. There are four kinds of sentence structure or, to put it
another way, four degrees of structural complexity. A sentence can
be simple, compound, complex, or compound-complex.

This is a *simple* sentence. Here are some more: 'It's a fine day.'
'Christmas is coming.' 'Mind the gap.' 'Love laughs at locksmiths.'
These sentences are called simple because in each of them there is
only one clause, which expresses a complete thought. This sort of
clause, which can stand by itself, is known as a principal clause.

A *compound* sentence contains two or more principal clauses.
Take, for instance, this sentence: 'The workers are angry and they

have gone on strike.' Here are two principal clauses, each expressing a complete thought. 'The workers are angry' is one such clause; 'and they have gone on strike' is the other.

A *complex* sentence contains one principal clause and one or more subordinate clauses, i.e. clauses which don't express a complete thought and therefore can't stand on their own but qualify, or modify, the principal clause. Example: 'The workers will go on strike unless they are given more money.' Here the principal clause, expressing a complete thought and capable of standing by itself, is 'The workers will go on strike'. The subordinate clause is 'unless they are given more money'.

Lastly, a *compound-complex* sentence contains two or more principal clauses and one or more more subordinate clauses. Example: 'The workers are angry and they will go on strike unless they are given more money.' Here 'The workers are angry' is one principal clause'; 'and they will go on strike' is another principal clause; and 'unless they are given more money' is a subordinate clause.

Now, a mixture of simple, compound, complex, and compound-complex sentences holds the reader's attention much better than a long unvaried string of one type alone.

The last six paragraphs may strike you as formidably technical. If so, take comfort from the fact that writers never consciously analyse in this way every sentence they write. There's no need to. Once you've grasped the idea that this sort of grammatical distinction exists you can cheerfully kick the ladder away by dismissing the details from your mind. Varying the length of your sentences will almost certainly lead to your varying their structure as well. Besides, there's another way of classifying sentences which, once you grasp it, will also make for variety in your writing. This is the distinction between loose and periodic sentences.

A *loose* or conversational sentence is one in which the main statement comes first and then further details are added. Example: 'Hundreds of workers marched with their banners along the road from the factory to the town centre.'

By contrast, in a *periodic* sentence you have to read to the end before the main statement is complete. Example: 'Along the road from the factory to the town centre, hundreds of workers marched with their banners.'

Periodic sentences differ from loose ones in three ways. They have a more formal feel to them; they place emphasis on the part of the sentence that precedes the main statement; and they create a feeling of suspense. While an unbroken series of one or the other type sooner or later becomes monotonous, a mixture of loose and periodic sentences helps to catch and hold the reader's attention.

Sentences are made up of words, and in the previous chapter we saw one way in which words can be classified. Another way of classifying them is as 'parts of speech': nouns, verbs, adjectives, adverbs, and so on. Generally speaking, if you want to make your writing clear and readable you should go easy on the adjectives and adverbs. Piling them on in a single sentence often results in making a piece of writing flabby and overblown. Don't try to impress your readers. Verbosity doesn't impress them; it puts them off.

Always remember that one appropriate, well-chosen adjective or adverb in the right place works far harder for you than a dozen of them peppered indiscriminately on your text. Putting it the other way round, remember that verbs, nouns, and pronouns make a sentence strong, whereas adjective and adverbs, if a sentence contains too many of them, can fatally weaken it.

Your sentences should sound pleasing to the ear, and it's never a bad idea to read them aloud at the revision stage. Sometimes hearing what your writing sounds like shows up a fault which is notoriously hard to spot otherwise but quite easy to cure when you do spot it: excessive repetition of the same sound.

This is often caused by strings of words all ending in '-ation', creating a jingle. In 1929 Samuel Beckett and others published a collection of essays on the book by James Joyce that was later known as *Finnegans Wake*. They called their collection *Our Exagmination round his Factification for Incamination of Work in Progress*. This jingle was deliberate; you should try to avoid producing such an effect accidentally. A similar fault, which the eye often misses but the ear soon picks up, is to let alliteration run to more than two consecutive words or to write this kind of thing: 'The demonstration was banned. Over 80,000 people with band and banners defied the ban' (Peter Fryer). This ugly-sounding passage could have been mended by putting 'prohibited' in place of 'banned' and 'prohibition' in place of 'ban'.

4

HOW TO PUNCTUATE

A sentence is brought to a close by means of a full stop, a question mark, or an exclamation mark—or occasionally, as we have seen, a dash, to indicate that it has been broken off unfinished. Within each sentence other kinds of stop may be needed to hold the sentence together and make its meaning as clear as possible. Just as carpenters and joiners have to know what kind and size of nail or screw to use for a specific purpose, and how best to use them, so writers have to know about the different kinds of stop that are available and how best to use them. They have to know when a stop is needed and which stop is the right one for any given job.

The comma
This is by far the most frequently used stop. It is also the one most frequently misused. Unfortunately it's difficult to draw up hard-and-fast rules about its use. To all such rules there are a great many exceptions; besides, many aspects of the comma's use are a matter of personal taste. It's easier, and no doubt more useful, to point to some of the mistakes that writers tend to make, either by leaving out a comma where there ought to be one or by putting one in where it's not needed.

You should try to use commas logically as far as you can. In particular, you shouldn't leave out one of the pair of commas that is needed for the job of enclosing, and thereby setting off, a parenthetic word or phrase. (A parenthetic word or phrase is one which, if you drop it from the sentence, leaves the rest of the sentence making sense.) By omitting one of such a pair of commas you are obscuring the structure of the sentence. Here are some examples of this very common error:

'But most sobering of all, winds of hurricane force regularly slam into northwest Scotland and the Shetlands' (Paul Simon). There should be a comma after 'But', corresponding to the one after 'all'; this pair of commas then clearly marks off the parenthetic phrase 'most sobering of all'.

'But after his suicide, he became reviled as a ruthless charlatan' (*Guardian*). There should be a comma after 'But', corresponding to the one after 'suicide'; alternatively, both should be omitted.

'But morals apart, there are aesthetic grounds for keeping sex low-key' (*Guardian*). There should be a comma after 'But', corresponding to the one after 'apart'.

'Stick to the classics, which people only pretend to have read, and if caught out, call it homage' (Maggie Traugott). The parenthetic phrase is 'if caught out', not 'and if caught out'. So there should be a comma after 'and'.

'Two writers, trapped in each other's company would almost certainly discuss money' (Nancy Banks-Smith). There should be either a comma after 'company', to correspond to the one after 'writers', or else no comma at all.

'The Queen made that mistake and even for a woman accustomed to being nipped around the ankles, it must cost her a twinge or two' (Nancy Banks-Smith). A comma should be inserted after 'and', corresponding to the one after 'ankles'.

'Greece has a Ministry of Culture as indeed, one would expect' (John Silverlight). There are three possible choices here: a comma before 'indeed', corresponding to the one after it; or one comma only, but after 'Culture', not after 'indeed'; or else no comma at all.

'Only when houses are seen as places to live and not as a means of making money, will the problems disappear' (R. Margrave). There should be a comma after 'live' ('live in' would be more idiomatic), corresponding to the one after 'money'.

'There was no such booking and to the best of British Airways' knowledge, there were no military personnel on the flight' (Mervyn

Walker). There should be a comma after 'and', or else no comma at all.

'He is the only man she has ever really loved, and terrified of losing him forever, she allows him to draw her back' (Simon Hoggart). The comma after 'loved' should come after 'and', to mark off the parenthetic 'terrified of losing him forever'.

'For Ms Ruthven to compound the error—rather lazily, and I dare say, unthinkingly—may also serve his review' (Edward W. Said). The comma after 'lazily' should come after 'and', or else there should be no comma at all.

'This reader found a good deal of Day's essay unintelligible, and where intelligible, not illuminating' (Richard Jenkyns). The comma after 'unintelligible' should come after 'and' instead. Better still, though, to rewrite thus: 'This reader found a good deal of Day's essay unintelligible, and where it was intelligible it was not illuminating.'

'At lunch though, it becomes apparent that not everybody here is cast from the same mould' (Jim Reid). There should be a comma before 'though' corresponding to the one after it. In this sentence it would be misleading to drop both commas, since 'though' might then be misread at first glance as a conjunction.

'He must realise, however, that the American Express advertisements—for which he was not paid incidentally—will leave him an even more obvious target' (Andrew Billen). The omission of the comma after 'paid' alters the sense of the phrase between dashes.

I have given plenty of examples of the illogical—i.e. misplaced or wrongly omitted—comma because this is by far the most common punctuation error. It is an error that careful writers do their best to avoid.

The next most common error in the use of commas is the weak comma: one that is used to join two parts of a sentence but isn't strong enough for that job. This leads to what is often referred to as the 'run-on sentence'. There are three possible cures: split the sentence in two; or use a semi-colon (or sometimes a colon) instead of the comma; or insert 'and' (or sometimes 'so') after the comma. Here are some examples:

'A smoker simply smokes, his motives and reactions are invisible and therefore incomprehensible' (Sally Vincent). The comma here should be a semi-colon; or a new sentence should start at 'His'.

'The trouble has only just begun, it will get much worse' (Michael Barber). Here again, a new sentence should start at 'It'; or the comma should be a semi-colon; or 'and' should be inserted instead of the comma.

The next three examples could each be mended in the same way: 'A cream-coloured Rolls-Royce pulls in, the occupants soon disappear into the throng of the foyer' (Jan Moir). 'The sculpture itself is not in the exhibition, it was considered too fragile to be shifted' (Fiona MacCarthy). 'About 250,000 people are dysphasic, 30,000 are added to their number every year' (Ruth Coles). Note however that if the last example is mended by splitting the sentence in two, most printers' and publishers' house-styles would rule that the second sentence should start, not with a figure, but with 'Thirty thousand'.

'If all else fails, you could emigrate to New Guinea, morning sickness is virtually unknown—there, boils are symptomatic of early pregnancy' (Sue Brearley). Suggested rewrite: '. . . New Guinea, where morning sickness is virtually unknown and boils are symptomatic of early pregnancy.'

'Like all of us, he [the Lord Chancellor] finds peeling the fruit rather annoying, all that stickiness and mess' (Jonathan Freedland). The comma here should be a colon or a dash.

'Such poetry does not work best through syllogism, it needs a leap across the excluded middle, or a simple placing of things' (*Times Literary Supplement* 'In Brief' review). The first comma here should be a semi-colon; or a new sentence should start at 'It needs'.

'Busoni praised her, even the satirical Thomas Beecham capitulated' (Noel Annan). The comma should be a semi-colon or should be replaced by 'and'.

'In the first place, the task itself is not grim, there is a singularity in Hardy, a skilled quirkiness, even if his angle of approach is predictable' (P.J. Kavanagh). The second comma should be a semi-colon; or a new sentence should start at 'There is'; or the word 'for' could be inserted before 'there is'.

'Books are clearly essential to study, it often takes longer to obtain books from the library than to read them' (*Guardian* letter). The comma should be a semi-colon, or a new sentence should start at 'It'.

'Islanders are used to referring to the German occupation in discreet asides, my bluntness got me nowhere' (Madeleine Bunting). The comma should be a semi-colon, or a new sentence should start at 'My'.

'Work for the controversial Child Support Agency will be a fresh challenge, it's too soon to say what the problems will be' (Peter Carty). The comma should be a semi-colon, or a new sentence should start at 'It's'.

'On the second visit they were luckier, the doctor who lived there was at home' (Peter Carty). The comma should be a semi-colon or colon, or a new sentence should start at 'The doctor'.

One last example, not quite so clear-cut: 'There is a great deal of violence in the books, people go mad, commit suicide, suffer obsessional passions' (Julian Symons). This would be improved by starting a new sentence at 'People' or by replacing the first comma with a semi-colon or colon.

There is a third quite common error in the use of commas: putting one in where it's not needed. A comma is certainly needed where, without it, the sense might be misunderstood at first glance, e.g. 'In the valley below, the houses looked tiny'. And a comma is certainly needed where without it the sentence would have a different meaning, e.g. 'He did not attend the meeting, because he had to baby-sit.'

These commas have the clear purpose of avoiding ambiguity; but in the next three examples, where there is no danger of ambiguity, the comma serves no purpose and should be left out.

'I strolled to the couch and lay down for what we call in the industry, the fiction writer's power nap' (Emily Prager).

'A high proportion of the costs Lynne Griffiths is now stuck with,' will go into Cherie Booth's pocket' (Leslie Caplan).

'The impact of such stomach-churning minutiae in this densely-packed but most agreeably pedagogical study, is to remind us of how much we have taken for granted in the very act of dining' (Jonathan Keates).

'Yet the works which define the orbit of Schubert's genius . . . were produced in the latter years, after Schober's dissipations had both interrupted the flow of Schubert's work, and diverted it into new channels. . . . ' (Ian Bostridge). It's the second comma, after 'work', that is unnecessary.

'How convenient to divide life into "the normal" on the one hand, and the illicit, irregular and deviant, on the other' (Cathy Star). There is no need for either the comma after 'hand' or the one after 'deviant'. (This sentence would be better still without 'and'.)

'In her lifetime, Maria has gone from being a member of the core of the Hungarian empire, to a member of an oppressed minority' (Catherine Field). Neither of these commas is necessary, and a careful writer would prefer '. . . to being a member of an oppressed minority'.

Some writers put an unnecessary comma after an adverb when that is the first word of a sentence. Examples: 'Recently, I had to open a concert at St Martin's in the Fields' (Norman Stone). 'Often, inspectors have nothing more to work on than a tip-off from a member of the public' (Christopher Middleton). 'Soon, I shall be able to flirt with psychotherapists in São Paulo' (Dulcie Domum). 'Sometimes, the best ideas are the simplest' (Melanie Phillips). These commas after 'Recently', 'Often', 'Soon', and 'Sometimes' do no work at all and should be left out. Similarly with a comma after an introductory 'Thus' or 'Therefore', unless of course that comma precedes a parenthetic clause which is closed off by a second comma (e.g. 'Therefore, as I told you, I had to rewrite the whole article').

A fourth error which careful writers try to avoid in their use of commas is to confuse the two distinct kinds of relative clause (i.e. a clause beginning with 'who', 'which', 'when', or 'where'). One kind is known as the 'defining' relative clause: 'The person who borrowed my umbrella has not brought it back.' The other kind is known as the 'descriptive' or 'non-defining' relative clause: 'John, who borrowed my umbrella, has not brought it back.' It is wrong to put a comma before a 'defining' relative clause, as is here done twice: 'Maybe it was simply Mission Impossible to give credibility to a chairman, who is an embarrassment, and to a DG, who early on made an ass of himself and the BBC with his tax affairs and his gloomy gobbledygook' (Richard Brooks). The commas after 'chairman' and 'DG' suggest there are more than one of each and should be omitted. It is equally wrong to omit a comma before a 'descriptive' or 'non-defining' relative clause, as here: 'It is an indication of how the Kurdish struggle has been marginalized that there is probably more literature available on Kuwait, with its half million citizens, than there is on the Kurds who number more than 25 million' (Paul Lalor). There should be a comma after 'Kurds'; its omission suggests that there are Kurds other than those who number more than 25 million.

There is a fifth error in the use of commas: leaving out a comma before 'which' when it has no single antecedent, i.e. when it means 'a thing which'. For instance, in 'He fell out of bed this morning, which gave him a big jolt', the comma is obligatory.

Before leaving the comma, let's answer three questions that beginners often ask.

1) *Should I put a comma before the final 'and' or 'or' in a list?*

Whether or not you insert such a comma ('She teaches English, French, German, Italian, and Spanish'; 'I don't like onions, cabbages, or sprouts') is entirely up to you; but take care that your choice is consistent within a single piece of writing.

2) *Should I put a comma between short phrases or main clauses joined by the word 'and'?*

Usually there's no need for one. For instance, 'She paused a moment and then stood up' needs no comma after 'moment'. But a comma is needed to separate main clauses where the second clause isn't closely identified with the first. Example: 'Cars will turn here, and coaches will go straight on.'

3) *Need I put commas before and after adverbs and adverbial phrases?*

Generally speaking not, unless you want to give special emphasis to the word or phrase so enclosed or to suggest a reservation or afterthought. For instance, 'This unfortunately costs too much' needs no commas unless you want to emphasise the word 'unfortunately'. The word 'nevertheless' doesn't normally need commas round it, though many writers put one after it when it's the first word in a sentence, thus: 'Nevertheless, there is undoubtedly a truth buried in the myth' (Ian Bostridge). Better without the comma, it seems to me. The word 'however' rarely needs a comma after it unless it's the first word in a sentence or clause. When it's in that position the comma prevents ambiguity: 'I shall be out all morning; however, you can call this afternoon.' But '. . . you can however call this afternoon' where there's no possible ambiguity, has no need of a comma.

An example of an unnecessary comma after an adverbial phrase: 'After the breakup, he continued to write, but with less wild success' (Jill Neville). The first comma here is better omitted.

The semi-colon

This stop is largely falling out of use, and fewer mistakes are made with it than with the comma. A highly educated secretary once told me how her new boss had pointed scornfully to a semi-colon in a letter she had typed from his dictation and demanded: 'What's this funny-looking thing?' Yet the semi-colon can still be very useful in three main ways:

First, it links two parallel clauses that aren't linked by a conjunction, where a comma would be too weak. Examples: 'I cannot dig; to beg I am ashamed'; 'To err is human; to forgive, divine'.

Second, the semi-colon links a series of parallel clauses some of which contain commas. But when you use it for this purpose you should take care not to miss out the necessary semi-colon before the last of these clauses. There is such an omission in the following long sentence, and it is confusing to the reader:

> In addition to disestablishing the Irish Church, the Liberals in the 1860s and early 1870s had abolished compulsory church rates, the 'taxes on knowledge', religious tests for Oxford and Cambridge, and the purchase of commissions in the army; they had legislated on Irish land, and on education for England and Scotland; they had opened the civil service to entrance by competition and they had made capitalism relatively safe for the investor by introducing limited liability—all this in addition to their preoccupation with free trade finance, proper government accounting, minimum budgets, and retrenchment. (*The Oxford Illustrated History of Britain*, ed. Kenneth O. Morgan)

Clearly there should be a semi-colon after 'competition'. Another example from the same book: 'Here [i.e. in the Lowlands of Scotland], burghs, abbeys, and cathedrals were founded; castles were built and royal sheriffdoms formed in order to reduce the kingdom to manageable administrative units; royal moneyers began to mint silver pennies (enjoying parity with English sterling) and import duties were collected.' There should be a semi-colon after 'sterling)'.

Third, the semi-colon is the best way of separating the items in a list where one or more of the items runs to more than one word. But it may be confusing to use a semi-colon in this way if the list is enclosed within a longer sentence, thus: 'But I have hopes that tyros such as Patrick Jenkin's boy, Bernard; Michael Fabricant; and Lady Olga Maitland will provide the *gravitas*, beauty and brains' (Julian Critchley). This would be better with two dashes inserted, one after 'tyros' and the other after 'Maitland'.

The colon
The colon has five main functions:

1) It can introduce a quotation or direct speech, though its use in that way isn't obligatory and a comma will often serve just as well.

2) A colon can introduce a list (there's no need to add a dash).

3) By standing in for, or supplementing, some such verbal forerunner as 'namely', 'that is to say', 'i.e.', 'the following', 'as follows', or 'to sum up', a colon performs the function, as Fowler puts it, of 'delivering the goods that have been invoiced in the preceding words'.

4) A colon is used to separate main clauses when the clause that precedes it is complete in sense and construction, and the clause that follows arises naturally from the first part in sense though not in construction. Example (from R.E. Allen's *Oxford Writers' Dictionary*): 'The universe would turn to a mighty stranger: I should not form part of it.'

5) A colon is used to separate main clauses where there is a step forward from introduction to main theme, or from cause to effect, or from premiss to conclusion. Example (from Allen again): 'Country life is the natural life: it is there that you will find real friendship.'

Dashes and brackets

Though the dash should not be over-used, as it notoriously was by Queen Victoria and Emily Dickinson, it can be very valuable. It marks the complete breaking-off of a sentence. It also marks a break within a sentence, when you want to interrupt your thought and go off on a different tack, or pull the reader up with a jerk—or, as here, introduce an afterthought. The dash can stand for an omitted word. Sometimes it can replace the colon. But its most important function is, in pairs, to deputise for a pair of brackets around an interruption in a passage which is grammatically complete without it.

In this last function a pair of dashes is less formal than brackets, whose use tends to make a piece of writing harder to read. But do make sure that the second dash comes in the proper place, so that without the two dashes and what lies between them the sentence still makes sense. In the following example the second dash is wrongly placed; it should come after 'from', not after 'directly': 'The issue of whether Mr Robinson had any control over—or gained

directly—from the Guernsey-based Orion trust was not addressed'
(*Guardian*).

Take care also that any parenthesis, whether enclosed within
dashes or brackets or commas, is reasonably short and simple. A
long and complex parenthesis puts a strain on the reader and shows
that the sentence needs rewriting. Example: 'Neither the Germans
nor the French (President Mitterrand has been particularly
supportive to John Major, since the French are terrified at being
stuck in a cave alone with the Germans) want to see a lingering rift'
(Simon Hoggart). Many readers, by the time they get to the closing
bracket, have forgotten the subject of 'want' and are forced to go
back to the start of the sentence. Better to write: 'Neither the
Germans nor the French want to see a lingering rift; President
Mitterrand', etc. (For more examples of this kind of awkward
writing, see pp. 56-7 below.)

If you use a pair of dashes for this parenthetic purpose be careful
not to use a third dash in the same sentence. This is liable to confuse
the reader. To find three dashes in the same sentence is a danger
signal that should leap to the eye at the revision stage. 'Chris
Bohjalian's quiet suggestion—in a novel that is competent if not
particularly adventurous—is that it's a good thing to have that look,
just in case you need it—should you ever find yourself an innocent
on trial' (Sylvia Brownrigg). It would be better to replace the first
two dashes with commas. 'Only weeks after the Thai Government
threatened a trade ban against Britain—over a dictionary saying
Bangkok was known for having lots of prostitutes—a government
Minister was asked to resign yesterday—for hiring call girls for a
parliamentary thrash' (Andrew Drummond). Again, commas would
be better than the first two dashes. Here is a sentence that contains
four dashes:

The seventeenth-century Neapolitan writer Giambattista Basile—a kind
of Italian Rabelais—wrote some of the founding fairy tales of the modern
corpus, often in wildly mischievous and funny versions, but they're not as
widely known as they deserve because the pyrotechnics of his style—and
his dialect—make him difficult. (Marina Warner)

This would be improved by substituting commas for the first pair of dashes. Better still to split the sentence in two, with a full stop after 'versions'; both pairs of dashes could then be retained.

The brackets referred to so far are round brackets, which printers call parentheses. Square brackets are used for a quite different purpose: to enclose something you yourself are adding to a quotation by way of comment, correction, explanation, or translation. Some writers are too fond of sticking '[sic]' or '[sic!]' into their quotations from other authors; it's a quick way of saying 'Yes, he *did* write that, believe it or not.' This sneering '[sic]' can soon become a tic; you would be well advised to go easy on it.

The hyphen

The hyphen has several functions. It joins two or more words to form a single expression (e.g. get-at-able). It joins a prefix to a noun (e.g. anti-Marxist). In the so-called 'hanging hyphen' it represents a shared second element in all but the last word of a list (e.g. two-, three-, or fourfold; 12-, 13-, and 14-year-olds). And it separates two similar consonants or vowels in a word, to help understanding and pronunciation (e.g. co-operate, Ross-shire, sword-dance).

But the hyphen's main use is to prevent ambiguity and make for clarity. Thus it separates a prefix from the main word when necessary (e.g. re-cover as distinct from recover, re-signs as distinct from resigns). A dancing girl isn't necessarily a dancing-girl; a poor rate-collection isn't necessarily a poor-rate collection; a black-cab driver isn't necessarily a black cab-driver; a little used car isn't necessarily a little-used car. A hundred odd spectators isn't the same thing as a hundred-odd spectators; a great grandfather isn't always a great-grandfather. 'Tree-climbing foxes', 'goods-carrying vehicles' and 'fox-hunting squires' look strange without their hyphens. Stranger still is such a sentence as 'Near the hotel is a moor reserved for shooting visitors'—until we put the necessary hyphen between its last two words.

There are no hard and fast rules about hyphenating compound words, but failure to do so when the first part of the compound already has another word tacked to it by means of a hyphen may look pretty odd. Take, for instance, 'Sweetest of the refuseniks was actress-cum-cake shop owner Jane Asher' (Barry Hugill). 'Actress-cum-cake' is abominable. If you don't care for multiple hyphens ('actress-cum-cake-shop-owner'), your remedy is to re-write the sentence: 'Sweetest of the refuseniks was Jane Asher, actress and owner of a cake-shop'.

Beware of the unnecessary hyphen. Some writers stick a hyphen between an adverb and the adjective it qualifies ('a neatly-dressed person', 'a beautifully-delivered speech', 'a richly-embroidered waistcoat'). But there's no need for a hyphen there. With such expressions as 'well known' the rule is simple. When they come before the noun ('attributively') a hyphen is needed ('a well-known politician', 'a well-thumbed book'). When they come after the noun ('predicatively') there is usually no ambiguity and so no need for a hyphen ('that politician is well known', 'this book is well thumbed').

One minor error, both frequent and irritating, is to use a hyphen in place of the word 'to', thus: 'Ian Gilmour served in Margaret Thatcher's Cabinet from 1979-81' (*Observer* strap-line). Without 'from', and with a comma after 'Cabinet' or with brackets round the dates, there would be nothing wrong with this; but 'from' makes all the difference since it implies a subsequent 'to'. So a careful writer would prefer '. . . served . . . from 1979 to 1981'. Similarly, 'From Wednesday-Friday will be mild' (*Independent* weather forecast) really will not do: the hyphen should be replaced by 'to'.

This chapter has had more to say about errors of punctuation and how to avoid them than about general principles of punctuation, which are hard to define and, frankly, pretty tedious. Unless you are making a special study of the subject you can probably get by with two such general principles:

1. Punctuation is best when it is determined by, and therefore clarifies, the structure of the sentence. The only valid exception to this general rule is where extra stops are needed to emphasise a particular word or phrase.

2. Don't use more stops than you need to make your meaning clear.

5

HOW TO WRITE A PARAGRAPH

The word 'paragraph' has two distinct meanings. What you should understand by it depends on whether you are writing for a newspaper or not. Most newspapers adopt the convention of using short paragraphs. Generally speaking these should be only a sentence or two in length, rarely more. They should seldom run to more than 40 words, never to more than 50. There's a good reason for having such short paragraphs in the narrow columns of newspapers. Research has shown that this convention makes for easy reading: it gives readers frequent breathing-spaces and encourages them to go on reading, whereas longer paragraphs look dull and forbidding.

But in books and many magazines a different convention is adopted: that of the 'topical' or logical paragraph. This is a unit of thought treating a single topic in a single sentence and thus enabling the writer to make clear, and the reader to grasp, the logical divisions of the thought. Though this convention usually makes for longer paragraphs than those in newspapers, the purpose of dividing the text into paragraphs is just the same. A new paragraph gives readers a breathing space. By breaking up the text in this way the writer is in effect saying to readers: 'Are you with me so far? If so, I'll carry on with the next point.'

How long should a paragraph be? This question is like asking how long is a piece of string. A paragraph, in the non-newspaper sense in which we're now using the word, is a unit of thought, not of length. There are times when a short, even extremely short, paragraph is appropriate. It is often a good way to provide a transition; in conversation, it indicates a change of speaker; it can give necessary emphasis to a particular example; not least, it is useful for summarising, introducing, or recapitulating an argument.

When a paragraph turns out to be longer than a printed page—i.e. more than about 400 words—a considerate writer usually prefers to chop it in two. And this is legitimate, since a printed page with no paragraph break looks forbidding. But it is not a good idea to do the opposite by stitching together two or more short paragraphs which lack unity of thought. That is liable to confuse and mystify readers.

Writers should beware of both a succession of very long paragraphs and a succession of very short ones. Such extremes often indicate a failure to plan. They may suggest that a writer has failed to think carefully enough about what needs to be said and, in particular, has failed to separate his or her thought into its logical divisions.

Just as a sentence is a properly arranged group of words, so a paragraph is a properly arranged group of sentences. Within each paragraph a careful writer tries to achieve a certain amount of variety. For a paragraph made up entirely of long sentences tends to grow monotonous. So does one made up entirely of short sentences.

Generally speaking, the guideline for both the first and the last sentence of a paragraph should be: the shorter the better. But this guideline must never become a fetish. If all your paragraphs are built on precisely the same pattern the variety you are striving for within paragraphs will elude you in the article or chapter as a whole.

How do you make a smooth and clear transition from one paragraph to the next? The resources available to you for doing this —the 'hooks', as it were, that join your paragraphs together—are of two kinds: mechanical and organic.

Mechanical transitional devices include such verbal work-horses as 'then', 'next', 'however', 'yet', 'moreover', 'all the same', 'on the other hand', 'at the same time'. Such expressions help to show relationships between elements that at first may seem unconnected. But they should not be used too regularly or be made too prominent by routinely appearing at the start of each paragraph's first sentence. Other mechanical transitional devices include repeated words, repeated phrases, and repeated sentence patterns. These too can all be very useful; but you should take care not to employ them carelessly or work them to death. Above all they should never be used in an attempt to join two paragraphs—two units of thought—which don't belong together. That's a recipe for failure.

Organic transitional devices are those which arise logically from the flow of your argument. One example is comparison and contrast, where you discuss what two writers, or two historical events, or two political positions, or two scientific discoveries, or indeed any two phenomena, have in common and what are the differences between them. One paragraph might summarise the similarities; a second, the differences. Or, in a longer piece of writing, each specific similarity or difference might merit a paragraph to itself. Another organic transitional device is known as 'partition'. This is where a writer divides the subject, or one aspect of it, into its component parts and then discusses each part in detail.

If your thought flows logically from one paragraph to the next you may not need any mechanical transitional device at all: the 'hook' is already there. Usually however a combination of mechanical and organic transitional devices is needed. Such a combination makes for smooth and coherent writing.

6

HOW TO WRITE AN ARTICLE

You can't pour a quart into a pint pot. This old saying may not long survive metrication, but the principle it states is good for all time and writers should constantly bear it in mind. So, before sitting down to write an article, find out first of all how long the editor wants it to be. Or, if you're submitting an article that hasn't been commissioned, study the publication you're writing for and work out for yourself what sort of length is suitable.

Nothing is more calculated to make editors tear their hair out in handfuls than a 5,000-word article submitted to a publication whose normal upward limit is 2,000 words; or a contributor who, invited to write 1,000 words, blithely turns in 1,500. Conversely, if your piece comfortably fits the space a busy editor has available it will make an excellent first impression. Mind you, that in itself doesn't guarantee acceptance. But first impressions do carry some weight, which is why writers are always well advised to submit copy that is double-spaced; to type or print on one side of the paper only; to give generous margins, allowing for plenty of editorial marks; to avoid inserts and last-minute corrections as far as possible; to number the pages; and to add their name, address, and telephone number at the foot of the final page. These elementary courtesies are the hallmarks of professionalism.

So the first rule of article-writing is: write to length. Word processors, their 'statistics' facility at call, make this far easier than it used to be; but, with or without this aid, writing to length should become a habit.

Having decided how long your article should be, your next job is to plan it. And here the first step is to make a heap. You do this by jotting down the points you want to get across in the article, just as they come into your head, as a list of catchwords or brief notes. After making the heap, you then have to organise it. This means arranging it in the most appropriate order, using the catchwords in your heap as headings, sub-headings and, if necessary, sub-sub-headings. Some people find that, for them, the best way of assembling the heap, or of putting it in order, is to use the non-linear form ('spider chart'), in which a key word is first put in the centre of a page and subordinate ideas branch out from it. For those who prefer it, this is the easiest and often the most fruitful way to start thinking about a topic.

Linear or non-linear, however you go about it, your aim is to provide yourself with a skeleton or ground-plan of the article. This ground-plan can be as simple or elaborate as you think fit, though obviously the shorter the article the less elaborate it needs to be. And, by the way, it will almost certainly give you a rough idea of how your article will divide itself into paragraphs.

French schoolchildren and British students on access courses are, I believe, taught to plan an essay so that it has a beginning, a middle, and an end. The beginning introduces the subject; the end is a summing-up; the middle is supposed to consist of a more or less systematic presentation of 'arguments for' and 'arguments against', with the essayist's answers to the latter. In general, the French essay tends to be rather more formal and structured than its English counterpart. But it's not a bad idea, at any rate in a polemical article, to take a leaf out of the French book and make sure you've dealt with your opponent's arguments systematically and haven't left a gap in your own argument. And in any article, polemical or otherwise, the beginning and end, or introduction and conclusion, are of special importance and should be given special attention.

Most important of all, perhaps, is the 'intro', as it's called in the trade. My one-time mentor Claude Cockburn ('Frank Pitcairn') used to say that, of the entire time available for writing an article, it's worth spending half on the 'intro'. This may be something of an exaggeration, especially when you're working to a tight deadline. But there's more than a grain of sense in Cockburn's advice, for it's based on a correct understanding of how people read.

The 'intro', above all else, should be an attention-getter. It should do what the Ancient Mariner did to the wedding-guest in Coleridge's poem: buttonhole readers, grab them by the lapel, make it hard for them not to go on reading. Your conscious aim in the 'intro' should be to make every reader sit up and take notice. It should be as crisp, punchy, and arresting as possible. For a dull 'intro' promises a dull article, and many readers, faced with a stodgy 'intro', simply stop reading and turn to something else that looks more promising.

With news stories the 'intro' is even more important than it is with other kinds of article, and I'll have more to say about this in the next chapter.

The conclusion to an article also needs special attention. It too should be punchy: summing up the article's main thrust in one or two crisp sentences, perhaps; or leaving a carefully thought-out question in the reader's mind.

In the course of planning your article in the way I have suggested, you will almost certainly come across one or two areas where you will need to look something up. It may be a fact or date that you're not sure about and therefore need to check; or the spelling of a person's name or of a place-name; or a quotation that needs to be verified, as quotations always do. Indeed you should *never* trust your memory on any of these matters. Memory can let you down, often when you least expect it and often with embarrassing results. The informed reader who finds a wrong date or a misquotation will be inclined to mistrust everything else in the article. So the planning stage is the time to look up everything that needs checking. Leaving this job until you've finished writing the article is bad workmanship. Checking facts, dates, spellings, and quotations isn't like putting on a coat of varnish; it's more like cutting each piece of wood to the proper size before fitting them together.

If you make a habit of laying down a solid foundation in this way—carefully planning what you're going to write, organising the material in the most appropriate way, and checking everything that needs checking before sitting down in front of the screen—you'll find that the actual writing goes smoothly. To return to our skeleton metaphor: if you have assembled the skeleton of your article in a thorough, skilful way, you'll find that the task of putting flesh on those bones can be a real pleasure. It's the people who don't plan and organise but improvise on the paper, sucking it out of their thumbs as they go, for whom writing is an ordeal.

Lastly, a few practical hints. Don't leave loose ends untied. Keep your promises. If you say you're going to discuss some aspect or aspects of your subject later on, don't fail to do so. If you say you're going to deal with four points, make it clear when you come to points two, three, and four. Never leave your readers in the dark about *who* did such-and-such, about *where* something happened, about *when* it happened. If you refer to a past event, tell your readers the year in which it happened—after checking it. If you quote the title of a book, check it and give the year of publication in brackets—after checking that as well. Anticipate and answer, as far as you can, obvious objections to what you're arguing.

In short, put yourself all the time in your readers' place. Meet them at least half-way. Make their path as smooth as you can. This isn't writing down—it's writing to communicate.

7

HOW TO WRITE A NEWS STORY

The annual general meeting of North Wessex trades council was held last Monday, with 70 delegates and 14 visitors present.

Would *you* go on reading a news item that began in such a dismally flat and boring way? Few people would. Most would skip at once to something that looked more interesting. And who could blame them?

A news story is a special kind of article, in which grabbing the reader's attention right at the start is even more important than it is with other kinds of article. With a news story, getting the 'intro' right is at least half the battle, and it's worth taking quite a bit of time and trouble over this.

In the first place, the 'intro' should be as crisp and punchy as you can possibly make it. This means, above all else, brevity. Try not to let your 'intro' exceed 30 words. If it runs to 40 words it's almost certainly too long, so have another go.

Beginners often feel obliged to cram a load of essential facts into the first paragraph. That's a mistake. All sorts of details—the full name of a trade union or other organisation, for instance, or an official's exact job title—can be left to the second or third paragraph (here the word 'paragraph' is used in the newspaper sense, as explained on page 35 above) or even inserted lower down.

In the second place, the opening paragraph should normally give the reader the gist of the news. (There's one exception to this, which I'll come to later on.) 'News' means something new, unusual, colourful, striking. There's an anecdote, no doubt apocryphal, about a young reporter on his first assignment, a meeting of the local council. He came back to the office to tell his news editor that there was no story.

'Why not?'

'The meeting wasn't held.'

'Why not?'

'Oh, they were just getting started when some chap in the public gallery pulled out a gun and shot the mayor dead.'

Maybe it's a cliché to say that 'dog bites man' isn't news but 'man bites dog' is. All the same, you can't write a news story about something that happens every day, something quite normal and unremarkable, unless you can get a fresh angle on it. Getting that fresh angle is just as essential in working-class journalism as it is for the capitalist press. And, by the way, those socialists who despise technique and professionalism as 'bourgeois' have a great deal to learn.

A punchy, newsy first paragraph not only grabs the reader's attention but can also be of great help to the harassed sub-editor who has to write a headline based on your story. If the 'intro' is good, the headline often almost writes itself.

I said there was an exception to the rule that the essence of the news should come in the first paragraph. This exception is the 'suspense lead', which can be no less an attention-grabber than the more straightforward kind of 'intro'. A 'suspense lead' keeps the reader guessing somewhat, until the second paragraph or even later. Here's a good example, from a news story by Charlie Pottins in *Workers Press*. The 'intro' read as follows: 'There was no mystery about the murder of 19-year-old Ivtasam Habashi.' I'm sure no one reading that 'suspense lead' would have failed to read the second paragraph too: 'Bound hand and foot and killed, her body shoved into an old car which was set alight, she was a sacrifice to "tradition" and "family honour".' Not until the third paragraph did the story give the victim's nationality, name her village, and say that she had been due to wed in a week's time and was pregnant by someone other than her fiancé.

This example shows how a 'suspense lead' can heighten a story's inherent drama by first arousing, then satisfying, the reader's curiosity. This is not a device which should be over-used; but used appropriately and skilfully it's a powerful shot in the writer's locker.

Once the 'intro' has been written, the rest of the story should be comparatively plain sailing. But there is one rule of thumb worth keeping in mind. Generally speaking, the more important facts and quotations should come higher up in the story, the less important ones lower down. In other words, a news story should be 'shaped' like an inverted pyramid. This matters to sub-editors who, working against the clock, may find that they have to cut one or more paragraphs out of your story to make room for some important news that has come in at the last minute. If they know for sure that they can cut from the bottom upwards this saves precious minutes, prevents their having to undertake time-consuming rewriting, and saves you from the discouraging feeling that your story has been mangled.

So this is one way in which a news story differs from other kinds of article: there need not be, and in fact there normally ought not to be, a conclusion, carefully planned to balance the 'intro'. For a news story is not, in structure or purpose, a kind of propaganda or agitational leaflet, concluding with a rousing call to action or a list of demands. The call to action or the demands, if worth their place, should be 'bled' into the body of the piece, not tacked on as an afterthought.

Once again, don't leave the reader guessing about any aspect of the story. Make sure that *who*, *when*, and *where* are made absolutely clear. Reread your story with a critical eye and check that you haven't left any loose ends untied. Check that you've spelt all names correctly.

Pay close attention to detail. Your readers will be glad if you do. Many a run-of-the-mill news story has been lifted out of the rut by the judicious use of a reference book. If you mention a town, state its population. If it's not a well-known place say how far it is from the nearest well-known city and in what direction. If you mention an MP, give his or her majority at the last election. Famous people often list their hobbies in *Who's Who* or give other revealing information about their lives, such as which West End clubs they belong to. *Whitaker's Almanack* will tell you how much a year their subscription costs. Such details, which can be looked up in a couple of minutes, can lend a little sparkle or piquancy to an otherwise humdrum story.

8

EIGHT KINDS OF BAD WRITING

Learning how to write well entails also learning how not to write. This chapter lists eight kinds of mistake that are often made. It gives examples of bad writing and explains why they are wrong and how they can be corrected.

1. 'Whom' for 'who' (and vice versa)

Slapdash writers often put 'whom' instead of 'who' where a parenthetic phrase comes between the relative pronoun and the verb of which it is the subject. This is an error, for 'whom' cannot properly stand as the subject of a clause: it has to be 'who'.

'For a president whom most people think is about to suffer the ultimate ignominy, he was admirably cool' (Hugo Young). There's a 'trick of the trade' you can use here—an easy way of finding out whether this is right. Remember that 'whom' corresponds to 'him' or 'her' or 'them', while 'who' corresponds to 'he' or 'she' or 'they'. So, in the present example, substitute 'him' for 'whom', miss out the parenthetic phrase between 'whom' and the verb, and see what it sounds like then. That gives us: 'him is about to suffer', which is obviously wrong. So it should be: '. . . *who* most people think is about to suffer', etc.

'A more fitting parade might have included . . . some of the 170,000 Iraqi children whom a team of Harvard doctors say will die within a year' (Andrew Stephen). Here our 'trick of the trade' gives us 'them will die'. So it has to be: '. . . *who* a team of Harvard doctors say will die', etc.

'He is full of praise . . . for the humble constable, "the lifeblood of the service" whom he feels is often ignored' (Duncan Campbell). Correction: '. . . *who* he feels is often ignored'.

'Among those who will lose their homes and land . . . are 5,000 Bosnians whom the Serbs claim have signed agreements volunteering to move. . . . ' (*Guardian*). Correction: '. . . *who* the Serbs claim have signed agreements', etc.

'Once again the people of one of Europe's poorest lands have chosen a president and a party whom many western commentators say are tainted and discredited by their communist past' (*Guardian* editorial). Correction: '. . . *who* many western commentators say are tainted and discredited', etc.

'Although she can be sharp about God, Muriel Spark is a keen admirer of the Holy Ghost, whom she feels has been seriously under-estimated' (John Mortimer). Correction: '. . . *who* she feels has been seriously under-estimated'.

'In Leeds Mark Lamarr was canvassing traffic jams and asking motorists to give a lift to The Laughing Swami, whom even Mark admitted was mad' (Nancy Banks-Smith). Correction: '. . . *who* even Mark admitted was mad'.

'Other factors in this desire to retreat from the world were his crippling stage fright . . . and his hatred of audiences, whom he believed were "out to destroy him" with the infectious microbes spread by their coughing' (Robert Craft). Correction: '. . . *who* he believed were "out to destroy him"', etc.

'Someone who at that time wrote a column in the *Literary Gazette and Journal* called "Sights of London" . . . (and whom Richard Altick believes may have been the editor, William Jerdan) described her as "the fairy of your superstition in actual life"' (Gaby Wood). Correction: '. . . *who* Richard Altick believes may have been the editor', etc.

'X, whom as we gather is an ambitious fellow, is also at this stage a prudent one' (Andrew Motion). Correction: 'X, *who* . . . is an ambitious fellow', etc.

'Mr Goff said he supplied a stream of fictitious information in the hope of satisfying Det Sgt Gough, including details of a local grocer whom he claimed was importing heroin' (David Ross). Correction: '. . . *who* he claimed was importing heroin'.

It is no less careless, though less noticeable, to write 'who' where 'whom' is needed, as in the following examples: 'Those who we call publishers have become people who do no more than commission books' (Andrew Motion). Correction: 'Those *whom* we call publishers', etc. 'His is a complicated submission relating to the conflict of evidence between two police officers who he has not, himself, cross-examined' (*Evening Standard*). Correction: '. . . two police officers *whom* he has not', etc. 'Most of the fields are hired out to contract farmers who few of the locals know' (William Hobson). Correction: '. . . *whom* few of the locals know'. 'The marriage was allowed, to the young Greek who Crawfie persists in referring to as "the Viking"' (Jenny Diski). Correction: '. . . the young Greek *whom* Crawfie persists in referring to as "the Viking"'. This grammatical mistake is now extremely common in the spoken language, which no doubt explains why it is not very noticeable when it appears in print. It is a mistake all the same, and should be avoided in the written language.

2. Plural subject, singular verb

In a sentence whose subject takes the form 'X *and* Y' and is therefore plural the verb should be plural as well.

'Ian Bell's adulation of poll tax non-payment . . . and his praise for the Scottish National Party was well off the mark' (George Robertson). Correction: 'Ian Bell's adulation . . . and . . . praise . . . *were* well off the mark.'

'But his name and maxim survives' (*Guardian* editorial). Correction: '. . . name and maxim *survive*'.

'When is swearing and nudity acceptable on TV?' (*Guardian* strap-line). Correction: 'When *are* swearing and nudity acceptable', etc.

'The unity and continuity of conscious experience has been greatly exaggerated' (Galen Strawson). Correction: '. . . unity and continuity . . . *have* been . . . exaggerated'.

'The anger and indignation unleashed at yesterday's

extraordinary meeting in London was fully justified' (*Independent* editorial). Correction: '. . . anger and indignation . . . *were* . . . justified'.

'But it would be nice to think that I could have an effect on the way in which the arts and, in particular, the music scene is treated by the media' (Peter Donohoe). Correction: '. . . the arts and . . . the music scene *are* treated', etc.

'The delicacy and subtlety of this dish was matched by only two other factors' (Ken Livingstone). Correction 'The delicacy and subtlety . . . *were* matched', etc.

'British red tape and hostility forces couple to adopt El Salvador babies' (*Observer* headline). Correction: '*force*', not 'forces'.

"Of course he was "cautioned" but it is of no effect if the nature and persistency of the questioning demands an answer' (Michael Mansfield). Correction: '. . . if the nature and persistency of the questioning *demand*', etc.

'The food and drink is supposed to be used to feed the thousands of people expected to attend the funeral' (Cindy Shiner). Correction: 'The food and drink *are* supposed to be used', etc.

'The mystery and spirituality of life is lacking' (Linda Grant). Correction: '. . . *are* lacking'.

This mistake is harder to spot when the verb, or part of it, precedes its subject: 'Only in the past 40 years has medicine and improved social conditions had a dramatic impact' (Chris Mihill). Correction: '*have*', not 'has'.

Occasionally the opposite mistake—singular subject, plural verb—is seen, as in 'The interest in psychoanalysis, psychology, counselling, psychotherapy and self-help have created whole new sections in the book shops' (Susie Orbach). Here 'have' should be 'has'.

3. Changing horses in mid-stream
Slapdash writers often treat a noun as both singular and plural in the same sentence. It's better to stick to one or the other.

'When the *Daily News* was finally persuaded by right-wing readers and by MI5 to dispose of their "Bolshevik" correspondent, he moved over to the *Manchester Guardian* (Paul Foot). Correction: either '*were* finally persuaded' or '*its* "Bolshevik" correspondent'.

'The Royal Shakespeare Company is selling their new production of S. An-ski's *The Dybbuk* as if it were a Yiddisher theme-park' (Clive Sinclair). Correction: either '*are* selling' or '*its* new production'.

'If London Zoo spends £15 per year on food for a single ant, I am not surprised at their predicament' (letter in the *Independent*). Correction: either 'If London Zoo *spend*' or '*its* predicament'.

'The Real Meat Company . . . has jumped forward to '92 in its processing arrangements, and their chickens are the ones I usually buy' (Richard Ehrlich). Correction: either '*have* jumped forward . . . in their processing arrangements' or '*its* chickens'

'The Merseyside authority has pursued the case despite the fact that, as it would probably themselves accept, it has largely lost the public argument' (Duncan Campbell). Correction: either 'it would probably *itself* accept' or '*have* pursued the case despite the fact that, as *they* would probably *themselves* accept', etc.

'The organised fraud section of the Benefits Agency has, we're told, "opened their doors for the first time"' (Hugh Hebert). 'Has' should be '*have*'.

'A television crew was attacked and robbed here last week by a crowd which also did thousands of pounds of damage to their equipment' (Cal McCrystal). Either '*were* attacked' or '*its* equipment'.

'Our Royal Family needs all our support and prayers in their current difficulties' (Barbara Cartland). Either '*need*' or '*its* current difficulties'.

'But the cultural Left also traffics in surrogate politics, which is why their fight with the conservatives resembles an exchange of paper bullets' (Dennis Wrong). Either '*traffic*' or '*its* fight'.

An inconsistency of another kind is to vary unnecessarily one's choice of preposition, thus: 'This leaves me awe-struck, both at the lavish resources of that medium-grade mid-western university and with the flattery implied in their devoting so much of them to turning the searchlights into the crevices through which Liberal

England stumbled to its strange death' (Roy Jenkins). This writer is awe-struck first *at* something then *with* something else; better to stick with 'at'.

The writer who uses 'the former' should be consistent by following it with 'the latter' instead of switching to a personal name, as in this sentence: 'Trotsky and T.E. Lawrence were perhaps the most outstanding of the intellectual activists to emerge from the first world war—the former as Lenin's principal executive, Lawrence as the delicate scholar and recluse, a Shakespearian Fortinbras materialising in the Arabian desert' (Saul Bellow). Better to write 'the latter' rather than 'Lawrence', or alternatively to write 'Trotsky' rather than 'the former'.

Yet another kind of inconsistency is sometimes seen in lists, when a writer uses the definite or indefinite article with one or more of the items but arbitrarily omits it with others, thus: 'I would not wish to give the impression that I am a lager lout, bitter bore or an ale arse' (Jools Holland). Correction: either insert 'a' before 'bitter' or delete the 'an' before 'ale'. This is a special case of the fault known as 'bastard enumeration' (see pp. 57-9 below).

When you use 'first' in a list you should not follow it with 'secondly', as here: 'There are at least two things wrong with this judgment. First, Kennedy gets off very lightly. . . . Secondly, do we really buy the idea that JFK invented the world of spin doctors and media manipulation?' (Desmond Christy). 'Second' is preferable—and, in general, 'first', 'second', 'third', etc. are better than 'firstly', 'secondly', 'thirdly', etc.

4. Wasting words

This fault takes various forms. It's a waste of words to say essentially the same thing twice over, thus: 'By fortuitous coincidence, *Newsnight* sent Mark Easton to Denmark' (John Naughton). 'Fortuitous' means happening by chance and is therefore unnecessary here; perhaps the writer meant 'fortunate'.

'Now priced less, too', says an advertisement. Perhaps 'Now cheaper, too' seemed too simple, or too cheap?

Another way of wasting words is to write 'but which' or 'and which', especially in places where the relative clause already starts with the word 'which', so that 'but' or 'and' alone is needed. Examples: 'Smolin is much more modest, and in a sense honest, in inviting us to consider his proposals as a new way of looking at physics—one which is nevertheless highly conjectural, but which has some potentially attractive features' (Michael Redhead). Better: '. . . one which is nevertheless highly conjectural but has some potentially attractive features.'

'But which' and 'and which' are even more objectionable when preceded by 'that', not 'which', as the first word in the relative clause, thus: 'Astronomers believe they have found the mysterious "dark matter" that makes up more than 95 per cent of the universe but which has never been seen' (Steve Connor). Better: '. . . "dark matter" that makes up more than 95 per cent of the universe but has never been seen.' Another example: 'Here is a skin that has never walked on the wild side, has always taken its make-up off last thing at night and which subsequently remains as clear as a virgin's conscience' (Jan Moir). Better to omit 'which'. In the next example, the writer mixes 'that' and 'which' in an unsightly jumble:

> The Invisible Man is not the happiest of titles for a life-story that chooses to close its eyes to a mass of Wells material that is already on the record, and which looks but glancingly at incidents of which we would like to know more, not less, than has already been divulged. (Ian Hamilton)

Suggested rewrite: 'The Invisible Man is not the happiest of titles for a life-story that chooses to ignore the mass of Wells material already on the record and merely glances at incidents about which we would like to know more, not less, than has already been divulged.'

'But which' is probably most objectionable of all when it follows an adjectival phrase that in turn follows the noun it qualifies. This almost always makes for ungainly writing. 'They're that most dangerous of things—a well-equipped army without a clear objective, but which refuses to demobilise' (Donald Macintyre). Better: '. . . a well-equipped army which has no clear objective but refuses to demobilise'. 'These scripts are the products of minds geared to written examinations, but which often fail to cope with the task of spending years sifting through documentary and other evidence and making good sense of it all' (Geoffrey Alderman). Better: '. . . minds which are geared to written examinations but often fail', etc. 'Behind their efforts is a West African community-based organisation called Six S . . ., founded in 1976 and which, by the late Eighties, had more than 4,000 groups working in nine countries bordering the south Sahara' (David Nicholson-Lord). Better: '. . . which was founded in 1976 and, by the late Eighties, had more than 4,000 groups', etc.

The objection to 'but which' and 'and which' also applies to 'but who' and 'and who'. And even when it's not wasting words a construction like 'but who' is often awkward, as here: 'A portrait of Dame Ethel Smythe, somewhat neglected now, but who cut quite a swathe as a 19th-century composer, author, traveller and suff-ragette' (*Independent on Sunday* TV preview). Better: '. . . Dame Ethyl Smyth, who is somewhat neglected now but cut quite a swath', etc. Incidentally, Smyth (1858–1944), who spelt her surname thus, lived more than half her life in the 20th century; and *The Oxford Writers' Dictionary* recommends spelling the noun 'swath' and reserving 'swathe' for the verb. The writer or sub-editor who can't bother to get such details right is in the wrong business.

Finally, it's a waste of words to use 'abstract appendages', as they have been called, turning 'weather' into 'weather conditions', 'behaviour' into 'behaviour patterns', and so on. This fault has already been discussed in Chapter 2.

5. 'Danglers'

A participle at the head of a sentence automatically attaches itself to the subject of the following verb. So writers should either make the subject consistent with the participle or rewrite a sentence disfigured with a hanging phrase, or 'dangler', so as to get rid of the participle. Examples:

'Blessed with an understanding headmaster, the biggest problems the Smiths have had to face so far have been with the medical profession' (Susan Young). Were the Smiths' biggest problems blessed with an understanding headmaster? Hardly. So it should be: 'Since the Smiths are blessed with an understanding headmaster, the biggest problems they have had to face so far', etc.

'Having been twice married, and with two sets of kids, this announcement has caused some alarm among the more distant of my relatives' (Julian Critchley). It is unclear whether it is the writer or the more distant of his relatives who has been twice married and has two set of kids; at any rate, this cannot be said of an announcement, so the sentence is in urgent need of revision.

'I have listened to the radio adaptations over the years and, while admiring their skill, their appeal remains a mystery to me' (Russell Twisk). It is not 'their appeal' which admires their skill; so it ought to be 'while I admire their skill' or 'while their skill is admirable'.

'Quizzing a friend about this thorny issue, the comparative word that sprang to her lips was master' (Ann Wells). It is not 'the comparative word' that quizzes; so it should be: 'When I quizzed a friend', etc..

Other 'dangling' or unattached phrases, not involving participles, are no less awkward:

'A 28-year-old former public schoolboy, his first novel, *Night Over Day Over Night,* was entered for the Booker Prize' (Justine Picardie). Was his first novel a former public schoolboy? Hardly. Suggested rewrite: 'This 28-year-old former public schoolboy's first novel', etc.

'Like the sensible chap he was, Henry's money stayed safely in his pocket' (Julian Critchley). Was Henry's money a chap? Clearly not. So it has to be: 'Like the sensible chap he was, Henry kept his money safely in his pocket.'

'Originally a painter, his interest in cinema was sparked by seeing Bergman's *The Seventh Seal*' (*Observer*). Was Peter Greenaway's interest in cinema originally a painter? Certainly not. Suggested rewrite: 'He was originally a painter, and his interest in cinema was sparked by', etc.

'Once labelled "Miss Homebreaker of 1954" by a Hollywood scandal sheet, Grace's appetite for sex led her to affairs with a veritable Who's Who of the fifties. . . .' (*Guardian* TV preview). But it was Grace Kelly herself, not her alleged appetite for sex, that was thus labelled. Suggested rewrite: 'Grace's appetite for sex—a Hollywood scandal sheet once labelled her "Miss Homebreaker of 1954"—led her to affairs', etc.

'Part rebel, part prima donna, her [Jennie Lee's] natural home was the platform, the political stage' (Shirley Williams). But it is Baroness Lee of Asheridge herself, not her natural home, that is said to have been part rebel, part prima donna. Suggested rewrite: 'She was part rebel, part prima donna, and her natural home was the platform, the political stage.'

'In no way an admirable citizen, the hunt he [Neil Hamilton] inspires is not an attractive thing' (Edward Pearce). But it is Hamilton, not the hunt for him, that is not an admirable citizen. Suggested rewrite: 'He is in no way an admirable citizen, and the hunt he inspires is not an attractive thing.'

'A lanky former soldier, who lists parachuting as one of his hobbies, his contributions to parliamentary debate, when noticed at all, have sometimes suggested that he has too often landed on his head' (Andrew Rawnsley). There are several ways of putting this right. Here is one: 'This lanky former soldier lists parachuting as one of his hobbies; his contributions', etc.

'Still trying desperately hard to be sexy and interesting, her everyday uniform was an ankle-length crepe de Chine tea dress and a velour dressing gown' (Jan Moir). Suggested rewrite: 'She was still trying desperately hard to be sexy and interesting, and her everyday uniform', etc.

6. Biting off more than you can chew
Careless writers tend to write the first thing that comes into their heads and, failing to revise, produce sentences that are awkward, clumsy, and unclear. This typically happens when a phrase is inserted in the wrong place.

Here's an example: 'Morgan takes a, never properly explained, obsessive interest in the whereabouts of the Treibers' (Alan Ross). Dashes instead of commas would do something to improve this sentence, but not much. Better to recast it altogether: 'Morgan takes an obsessive interest, never properly explained, in the whereabouts of the Treibers.'

Another example: 'There is still a lot of biographical information (recently enhanced by the testimony of Soma Morgenstern, of which both *Companions* make full use) to be explored' (Hugh Wood). This needs drastic recasting: 'There is still a lot of biographical information to be explored; it has recently been enhanced by the testimony of Soma Morgenstern', etc.

A further example:

> The appendix that appeared in the first edition listing six categories of
> books that were related to items in the main catalogue, but distinct from
> them (such as books wrongly attributed to Catholics, and ghosts which
> appear in standard sources, but which apparently do not exist today), has
> been omitted. (P.R. Harris)

Suggested rewrite: 'An appendix appeared in the first edition listing six categories of books related to items in the main catalogue but distinct from them, such as books wrongly attributed to Catholics, and ghosts which appear in standard sources but apparently do not exist today. This appendix has been omitted.' (For 'but which', see pp. 51-3 above).

Yet another example, made still worse by the clumsy placing of the last two words: 'He [Aneurin Bevan] played a big role (one of the reasons the Conservatives hated him so) in rallying opinion in the Labour movement against continuing the wartime coalition under Churchill's leadership into peacetime' (Andrew Gamble). Suggested rewrite: 'One of the reasons the Conservatives hated him so was the big role he played in rallying opinion in the Labour movement against continuing into peacetime the wartime coalition led by Churchill.'

Even when it's in the right place the parenthetic phrase may be so long as to unbalance the sentence altogether, as we saw when discussing dashes (pp. 31-2 above). In the following example an insupportable weight is thrown on the final word: 'He made the work in which we were engaged and which was curiously testing because of the hostility it aroused, fun' (Mark Bonham-Carter). This is hardly fun to read and should have been rewritten something like this: 'The work we were engaged in was curiously testing because of the hostility it aroused, but he made it fun.'

The badly placed phrase need not of course be a parenthetic one. 'First among them in iconic power is Schwind's "Ein Schubert-Abend bei Joseph von Spaun", a picture which has transmitted that special notion of a concert for and among friends, a "Schubertiad", into the historical imagination' (Ian Bostridge). Much better to transpose the phrase 'into the historical imagination' so that it follows the word 'transmitted'.

A badly placed phrase sometimes tricks a writer into omitting a necessary word, thereby creating nonsense: 'The poor are watching as much, if not more, than ever' (*Independent on Sunday* editorial). As much than ever? The careless sub-editor would have done well to insert 'as' after 'much' and to have transposed the comma after 'more' so that it follows 'than'. Better still to recast the sentence altogether: 'The poor are watching as much as ever, if not more.'

A final example of a writer biting off more than he can chew, or overloading the cart—here not through a badly placed phrase but through having too many phrases in apposition: 'CC offered one of its best young lawyers, Margaret Palfrey, a pensions expert, every young lawyer's dream—a partnership' (Marcel Berlins). This is a nightmare of a sentence. Suggested rewrite: 'CC offered a partnership—every young lawyer's dream—to one of its best young lawyers, the pensions expert Margaret Palfrey.'

7. Bastard enumeration

'There is perhaps no blunder by which hasty writing is so commonly defaced', says Fowler of this kind of slovenliness, in which what is common to some of the items in a list is not common to all. We have already seen one example of this, on page 51. Here are some more:

'Those who never met him . . . would never have guessed at his charm, lovability, or his high intelligence' (A.N. Wilson). The word 'his' should be inserted before 'lovability'; or, alternatively, the 'his' before 'high intelligence' should be deleted.

'*Trollopiana*, the Society's journal, examines the personality of Phineas Finn, Trollope's low view of the press, and asks what Burgo Fitzgerald really felt about Lady Glencora' (Julian Symons). The comma after 'Finn' should be replaced by the word 'and'.

'He had a French cavalryman's moustache, a sergeant's voice, and was in the habit of being driven the wrong way around roundabouts by his confidential secretary' (Julian Critchley). There are two ways of putting this right: the comma after 'moustache' could be replaced by 'and'; or, alternatively, the words 'was in' could be deleted.

'Like all Auster's books, it's terribly poor in transcribed life, totally unobservant and has no sense of humour' (Philip Hensher). Insert 'is' before 'totally'.

'Rosemary Bailey dreams of drinks with Graham Greene, dinner with D H Lawrence and shares in the beauty that inspired a generation of jetset writers and artists . . .' (*Guardian* strap-line). Insert 'and' in place of the comma after 'Greene', and insert a comma after 'Lawrence'.

'Today Mark owns a £1 million house in Texas, a £2 million house in The Boltons in London and travels first class with his family and a butler in tow' (Henry Porter). Insert 'and' in place of the comma after 'Texas', and insert a comma after 'London'.

'Cage was America's best Dadaist, best Surrealist, best self-publicist, self-archivist, and its worst composer' (Paul Driver). Insert 'best' before 'self-archivist' and delete 'its'.

'Today, there are children unable to read or write properly; acts of brutality and bullying in the playground; there is crime, truancy and teenage pregnancy' (Loretta Loach). Delete the words 'there is' after the second semi-colon (and delete the unnecessary comma after 'Today').

'Both had grizzled and wiry hair, bright red faces and wore bright blue shirts' (John Wells). Replace the comma after 'hair' with the word 'and', and insert a comma after 'faces'.

An example of a different kind: 'The most expensive, longest-running and ridiculous election campaign of the decade will finally end in Monte Carlo at 7.20 BST tonight . . .' (Matthew

Engel). Here 'most' qualifies 'expensive' and 'ridiculous' but clearly cannot qualify 'longest-running', which is already in the superlative form. This 'bastard enumeration' could easily be corrected by inserting 'most' before 'ridiculous'.

8. 'You and I' for 'you and me'

'It may be, dear reader, time for you and I to find something to occupy them' (Henry Porter).

You can easily see what's wrong here if you miss out the words 'you and'. It has to be 'time for me', not 'time for I', so this sentence should read: 'It may be, dear reader, time for you and me to find', etc.

9

SIGNS OF A CAREFUL WRITER

In the previous chapter we looked at examples of out-and-out bad writing and how to avoid it. In the present chapter we are concerned with writing that is not so much bad as graceless. Here much depends on personal taste and there's little point in trying to lay down rigid rules. All languages are in constant change, and the English language has been changing at an increasing rate in the past 50 years; the written language has changed less than the spoken language, but it has changed all the same. The preferences expressed in this chapter are frankly those of a writer of the older generation, who regrets the disappearance of useful distinctions, finds certain novelties unpalatable, and views some recent changes in usage as solecisms. Some readers will certainly regard some of my preferences as old-fashioned; and I expect that most if not all of the novelties and colloquialisms I advise against will be regarded as normal in fifty years' time, just as 'radio' has supplanted 'wireless' in the past fifty years and 'anybody' has ousted 'any body' in the past 400. So all I can do is tell the reader the choices I think a careful writer should make towards the close of the 20th century. Whether you agree with me or not is up to you.

The careful writer, then, maintains certain useful distinctions that seem to be dying out or, at any rate, are becoming seriously blurred:

The distinction between 'less' and 'fewer'. 'Less' applies to quantity; 'fewer' applies to number. You can eat less butter, but you will put on fewer calories, not less calories.

The distinction between 'disinterested' and 'uninterested'.

Someone who is disinterested has no personal bias in a matter, so 'disinterested in' should not be used in the sense of 'indifferent to', as it is here: 'He is almost disinterested in the game, which ends in a 2-2 draw' (John Mullin). 'Uninterested' is preferable.

The distinction between 'due to' and 'owing to'. The use of 'due to' as a prepositional phrase or compound preposition strikes me as careless. 'Fischer defaulted a game due to a dispute over television cameras' (Leonard Barden). 'The term nudist is no longer in use, due to its nudge-nudge connotations' (Cressida Connolly). 'He lives in somewhat reduced circumstances due to his ill-fated venture in the West' (Hugo Williams). 'Surely a special cross should be made for Mr Waldegrave, otherwise known—due to his work on various charters—as the Citizen's Willie' (Andrew Moncur). 'Due to the decline in educational standards, the word "fatalism" is used sloppily by many' (Keith Boot). 'Security was tight due to the IRA threat' (*Observer* caption). 'There was . . . the occasion when, due to the late arrival of the 18.33 from Bexley Heath, a party of six theatregoers missed the show' (Sue Arnold). In each of these examples 'owing to' or 'because of' would be a careful writer's choice—though a sentence such as 'His reduced circumstances are due to his ill-fated venture', where 'due' is an adjective, is of course unobjectionable. *The Pocket Oxford Dictionary of Current English* now marks 'due to' with a **D**, indicating 'a use that, although widely found, is still the subject of much adverse comment by informed users'.

The distinction between 'compared with' and 'compared to'. To compare something *with* something else is to analyse their similarities and differences; to compare something *to* something else is to note a striking likeness between them. So, in '. . . the reduced type of both text and notes (as compared to most earlier titles in the *Collected Coleridge*)' (Norman Fruman), a careful writer would prefer 'with'. And a careful writer would substitute 'with' for 'to' in the following examples as well: 'Compared to his Prime Minister, the Chancellor has always shown a healthy scepticism' (*Observer* editorial); 'Compared to some of the other death metal outfits already performing and selling records in Britain, Dismember start looking kind of cuddly' (Zoë Heller); 'The reviews are scholarly, always comparing recordings to previous versions' (*Times Literary Supplement*); 'Compared to a twelfth-century country church, St Helen's Bishopgate in the City of London has had an eventful past' (Gillian Darley); 'Compared to his new friend he felt ugly, inept and woefully inexperienced' (Andrew Motion). 'Compared to their British counterparts, candidates are formidably well equipped for the struggle' (John Sutherland). 'Yes, I turn my back on petty, cliquish, victim-obsessed British feminists, who are small potatoes indeed compared to the real glories of modern British culture' (Camille Paglia).

But in the following four sentences a careful writer would substitute 'to' for 'with': 'This view is nearer the truth than the wild panegyrics of the Francoists who compared him with Alexander the Great, El Cid and Napoleon' (Paul Preston). 'When discussing Dulwich it's almost de rigueur to compare it with the Frick collection in New York as a museum of exactly the right size' (Waldemar Januszczak). 'If I felt even remotely charitable towards the series, I might even compare it with Gulliver's Travels' (Roy Hattersley). 'A column in Friday's *Washington Post*, echoing Clinton's belief, compared British policy over Bosnia with that of Neville Chamberlain's appeasement of Hitler' (Andrew Stephen).

The distinction between 'imply' and 'infer'. To imply something is to suggest it without saying it. To infer something is to deduce it, or draw it as a conclusion. 'Infer', like 'due to', is now marked with a warning **D** in *The Pocket Oxford Dictionary*.

The distinction between 'consist in' and 'consist of'. To consist *in* means to have its essential features in; to consist *of* means to be composed of. 'The greatest threat to the family consists of the pressure (economic and otherwise) on mothers to go out to work' (Richard Ingrams); this should be 'consists in'.

The distinction between 'between' and 'among', the first of which is properly used where two things or people are concerned; if there are more than two, 'among' is preferable. 'The entries poured in and it hasn't been easy choosing between them' (Jack Hughes). Here 'among' would be better.

Except where faithfully reporting conversation, careful writers
avoid such unidiomatic constructions as 'bored of' (for 'bored with')
and 'fed up of' (for 'fed up with'), which are rapidly gaining ground
in speech. Unidiomatic too are: 'Though Russ was forbidden from
contacting a lawyer on the boy's behalf' (Andrew Stephen) and 'She
was forbidden from working with any photographer other than
Bruce Weber in any clothes other than Calvin's' (Marion Hume). In
the first sentence 'forbidden to contact', in the second, 'forbidden to
work', is the normal idiom and therefore preferable.

Another departure from standard idiom, now extremely frequent,
is the use of 'like' as a conjunction, a colloquialism that carries *The
Pocket Oxford Dictionary*'s warning **D**. 'Perhaps he got bowled over
and stamped on by one of my mother's horses, just like I did six
years ago' (Kathryn Flett). The careful writer would prefer 'just as I
did'. 'I felt like I was getting ripped off' (Daisy Waugh). Preferable
is: 'I felt as if', etc. 'He looked like he had slept a little, cried a lot'
(David Harrison). Better: 'He looked as if', etc. 'Some boots are
made for walking. Others just look like they are' (*Observer*). Better:
'Others just look as if they are.' 'Some six years ago they . . . started
calling themselves the World Service, like everyone else always had'
(Anne Karpf). Better '. . . as everyone else always had'.

Yet another unidiomatic construction that is seeping over from
colloquial speech is the use of the past participle in contexts where a
careful writer would choose the present participle, as in: 'It is 9.45
before the two of us are safely stood with one foot on the windowsill
and the other on the booby-trap ladder we bought in 1986' (Phil
Hogan). The careful writer would prefer 'are safely standing'.

Careful writers avoid vogue words and vogue phrases such as
'hopefully' in its latter-day sense and 'more importantly' and 'most
importantly'. 'Hopefully' is objectionable because it wipes out point
of view; it doesn't tell us who is doing the hoping. 'More
importantly' and 'most importantly', which have spread across the
newspapers in the past decade or two, are objectionable mainly
because they take five syllables to convey the same meaning as
'above all' conveys in three. 'Third, and I suspect ultimately most
importantly, as her image as comic revenger shimmered across the

tabloids' front pages, she began to confront herself with the question of who, to speak the psycho-babble she despises, she was' (Andrew Billen). A writer with a sensitive ear would probably prefer something like this: 'Third, and perhaps above all, . . . she began to ask herself who she was, to use the psycho-babble she despises.' Another example: 'There is none of the autobiography dressed up as imagination, none of the fumbling language, flimsy structure or inadequate characterisation of lesser débuts; there is, most importantly, a good story' (Fiammetta Rocco), 'Above all' would be far better, as it would be in the following example: 'Their reward was to see their words reproduced in newspapers—and, more importantly, to be invited to say them again on TV and radio' (Ian Aitken).

Careful writers avoid ambiguity by changing the order of words in a possibly ambiguous sentence. 'She kept the wrist-watch he gave her all her life' (Claire Tomalin) is better rewritten thus: 'All her life, she kept' etc. 'Here I can speak from experience, having attended the lectures on which most of *Analysis and Metaphysics* is based as a student' (Colin McGinn). Rewrite: '. . . having attended as a student the lectures' etc. 'She has also written about being single in the Daily Telegraph' (*Evening Standard*). Better: 'She has also written in the Daily Telegraph about being single'. 'In the late 1950s, when I chose to lecture on the history of women at Oxford, most of my colleagues regarded the subject as bizarre' (Keith Thomas). Better: '. . . to lecture at Oxford on the history of women', etc. 'It might be tactful this week, what with all the excesses of the last few, to dwell on the delicious dinner I ate recently in as little detail as possible' (Daisy Waugh). Better: '. . . to dwell in as little detail as possible on the delicious dinner I ate recently'. 'I brought home some cherry tomatoes still attached to the vine from Italy last week' (Hugo Arnold). Better 'I brought home from Italy last week some cherry tomatoes still attached to the vine.' 'After managing to lose Germaine Greer you need a woman who knows her own mind rather urgently' (*Guardian* letter). Better: '. . . you rather urgently need a woman who knows her own mind'.

Careful writers don't run words together that should be kept separate: 'Before anyone writes into the Editor to complain about this extravagance . . . ' (Sue Arnold). This, which was perhaps a sub-editor's or printer's error, should read: 'Before anyone writes in to the Editor', etc. 'He couldn't say anymore because investigations were continuing' (Charles Nevin). This should be: 'He couldn't say any more', etc.

Careful writers avoid such illiteracies as 'lead' for 'led'. They avoid orthographic novelties like 'alright'. They avoid undue repetition of their own pet phrases. They avoid using trendy expressions they have lately seen widely used, unless their own use of them is unmistakably ironic.

Careful writers avoid anything that smacks of over-correctness, as in the following five examples: 'I play it with advertisements, by trying to guess at what sort of people they are aimed' (Greg Walker); here the natural thing would be to write: '. . . by trying to guess what sort of people they are aimed at'. 'The reader, disarmed by such frankness, might ask at what sort of audience Performances is directed' (Peter Gathercole). Far better would be: '. . . might ask what sort of audience Performances is directed at'. 'Not only are they able to translate their own work, they can choose in which language to write' (Carol Mansur). Better: '. . . they can choose which language to write in'. 'Dahmer himself appears so far sunk into his private pit that it would seem to make little difference in which sort of institution he spends the rest of his life' (Sebastian Faulks). Better: '. . . little difference which sort of institution he spends the rest of his life in'. 'The Labour party has its own reasons, at which one can only guess—if not with great difficulty' (*Observer*). Better: '. . . which one can only guess at', etc.

All five of these writers are tying themselves in knots so as not to end a sentence with a preposition. But this is a superstition, not a rule, and it often makes for clumsy writing. Avoiding at all costs an end-of-sentence preposition may be what caused the following ambiguity: 'What part of a man turns on women? His bum, according to most surveys in women's magazines' (Richard Brooks). Better: 'What part of a man turns women on?'

Another superstition, or shibboleth, is that adverbs have to end in

'-ly', and that such time-honoured idiomatic expressions as 'hold tight' and 'sure enough' need 'correcting' into 'hold tightly' and 'surely enough'. This leads to writing that comes over as pompous: 'Without a long, elitist tradition of art connoisseurship to call on, the new medium of representation doubtlessly seemed ideally suited to the evolving pragmatic and fluid society' (Peter Hamilton). 'Doubtless' is just as goodly an adverb as 'doubtlessly'—and here, closely followed by 'ideally', it would be preferable .

Careful writers think twice before using a foreign word or phrase where there is a perfectly adequate English equivalent. And if, after taking thought, they still feel the need to use the foreign word or phrase, they take pains to get it right—not, like the *Guardian*'s education correspondent, or perhaps a sub-editor, spelling *de rigueur* without the first *u*; nor, like Andrew Anthony or his sub-editor in the same newspaper, inserting a redundant *t* after the *n* in *événements* and dispensing with both accents.

Come to that, careful writers check and double-check all quotations, never relying on memory. 'Orwell says: "Kipling is almost a shameful pleasure, like the taste of cheap sweets that some people carry into middle life"' (Helen Chappell). But what Orwell does in fact say is rather different: 'Kipling is almost a shameful pleasure, like the taste for cheap sweets that some people secretly carry into middle life.'

Lastly, careful writers avoid giving words and phrases meanings they do not bear, as in: 'The real trouble with "link", I think, is that it's politically correct, implying that there's nothing to choose between the places connected. Which begs the question . . . Why not stay at home?' (Andrew Martin). To beg the question means to assume the truth of something which requires proof. The writer means 'Which raises the question', and that is what he should have written. A further example:

[H]ow . . . have we reached the stage where Government in the most powerful country on earth has ground to a stuttering halt on account of some rumoured fumblings by the President? Because the President is rumoured to have lied about the rumours? That, to be sure, is a serious matter in a legal context. But it begs the question: why, if he lied, did he feel the pressure to lie? (*Guardian* editorial).

The writer means 'But it raises the question', and that is what should have been written.

10

THE SELF-DISCIPLINE OF STYLE

Listen to John Major on *Desert Island Discs*, talking about his boyhood in south London: 'From time to time neighbours would *dispatch* me to place bets with an illicit bookie who *plied his trade in the environs of* Loughborough Station.' As somebody asked in the *Observer*, what's wrong with 'send', 'worked', and 'near'?

Major, in this stiff, pretentious sentence, reminds me of a great-aunt of mine. Having moved a notch or two up in the world by marrying a moderately prosperous local shopkeeper, she always put on a would-be posh voice when answering the telephone. In the spoken language, that kind of thing is both comical and trivial. My great-aunt's imperfectly 'improved' vowels and our former prime minister's pompous circumlocutions have both been blown away by the wind. But when people *write* in a would-be posh way, pretending to a social position or a *gravitas* or a wisdom that nature didn't give them, the printed result, while often comical, is less ephemeral and therefore less trivial. So the first, and perhaps the only golden, rule of style for an aspirant writer is: be yourself. 'Style is the man himself', said the eighteenth-century French naturalist Buffon. Nowadays, since 'man' no longer embraces 'woman', we'd have to put that rather differently, but the message is as valid as ever: everything in your writing that isn't straightforwardly and honestly your own inevitably comes across as affected, pretentious, or imitative. Writing is revealing.

Many young writers start out by imitating a writer, or several writers, whom they greatly admire. Such imitation may have some value as an exercise but, unless you're aiming to be a parodist, its value is limited. Some bogus 'Trotskyists' do indeed write in a way that reads like a parody of Trotsky, whose writings they have swallowed whole, in translations of varying merit, but have not digested. They write in ready-made phrases, laid end to end, which saves them the trouble of thinking for themselves. But they simply aren't capable of Trotsky's daring metaphors, or his passion, or his analytical power. So reading their formulaic writing is, as Trotsky used to say, like swallowing bristles.

You have to find your own voice. This means, above all else, self-discipline. Beginners have to realise that when they get to grips with style it is themselves and no one else they are getting to grips with. The better you know yourself—your strengths and weaknesses, your purpose and abilities—the better your writing will become, since the more honest and less contrived it will be.

It can hardly be emphasised too strongly that style isn't a kind of sauce that you ladle on your work in great dollops to make it palatable or piquant. You can't separate style from content in that way; and no amount of 'stylistic' tinkering will ever convert a dull piece into a sparkling one.

The self-discipline of finding your own voice means, above all, not adding anything but taking some things away. You have to steel yourself to cut certain things from your work quite ruthlessly. For a start, you have to cut out all those devices that people generally think of as demonstrating 'style': i.e. all mannerisms, flourishes, and bits of fancy writing. Everything purple, in fact. Finding your own voice means also cutting out all fashionable ready-made phrases, especially ones that you've seen rather a lot of lately. Such phrases tend to be copied from writer to writer, especially by journalists in a hurry, who habitually follow their leader like sheep, and they spread across newspapers like a rash. These fashionable ready-made phrases are not *your* voice, but the echoes of other people's voices.

So are all those dead metaphors that save you the trouble of thinking for yourself. These too should be pruned, rigorously. George Orwell, in his 1946 essay on 'Politics and the English Language' (reprinted in vol. 4 of his *Collected Essays, Journalism and Letters*), lists a great number: 'ring the changes on', 'take up the cudgels for', 'toe the line', 'ride roughshod over', 'stand shoulder to shoulder with', 'play into the hands of', 'no axe to grind', 'grist to the mill', and many more.

Lastly, in order to discover your own voice you would do well to dispense with those flabby, semi-meaningless phrases that replace simple verbs, conjunctions, and prepositions. Examples (some from Orwell again, others from Fowler): 'render inoperative', 'militate against', 'make itself felt', 'serve the purpose of', 'with respect to', 'having regard to', 'inasmuch as', 'in connection with', 'in order that', 'in the instance of', 'in the neighbourhood of'. Using phrases like these in your writing is like speaking to somebody through a soggy face-flannel, or with a mouth full of porridge. Fowler calls such phrases 'almost the worst element in modern English, stuffing up what is written with a compound of nouny abstractions'. And he adds:

> To young writers the discovery of these forms of speech, which are used very little in talk and very much in print, brings an expansive sense of increased power; they think they have acquired with far less trouble than they expected the trick of dressing up what they may have to say in the right costume for public exhibition. Later they know better, and realize that it is feebleness instead of power that they have been developing.

All this ruthless self-editing, I know from bitter experience, is asking rather a lot of the young writer. But the self-discipline it entails is an indispensable part of learning your craft, even if it does cut your ego down to size now and again. There's a bit of an egotist inside every writer. There has to be, if you're to work up the head of steam that's needed to get through the lonely task of arranging your thoughts coherently on paper. Half the battle, in learning to be a competent writer, is coming to terms with that ego—breaking it in and harnessing it, if you like, for the task in hand, which is not self-indulgent self-expression but communicating your thoughts to others.

So bear in mind the following observation: if you've written a sentence or a paragraph that you feel especially proud of, then probably—not certainly, but probably—it isn't worth the paper it's written on. Therefore either cut it out altogether or rewrite it drastically, preferably after doing what should really become a habit: putting the whole piece away in a drawer for as long as possible so that you can come back to it with a fresh mind and look at it with a newly critical eye, as if someone else had written it. This advice to 'murder your darlings' sounds harsh, and sometimes it takes courage to carry it out. But it's the single most useful piece of advice that was ever given to me as a young writer; it has stood me in good stead, and that's why I pass it on.

In your style of writing you reveal your personality, both consciously and unconsciously. If you care enough about your work to take pains to express yourself with honesty, clarity, and vigour, then your readers will respect you—however much you may irritate them sometimes.

11

SOME QUESTIONS ANSWERED

Here are the answers to some questions asked by readers of this booklet's first edition.

What about split infinitives?
Star Trek's original 'To boldly go where no man has gone before' was corrected for a later series. But it didn't become 'To go boldly', etc., or even 'Boldly to go,' etc. It became: 'To boldly go where no one has gone before.'

My advice is: emulate the *Star Trek* editors and don't agonise over splitting infinitives. Split them or not, as you choose. Like the shibboleth about not ending a sentence with a preposition, the ban on split infinitives was the brain-child of grammarians who thought 'classical' Latin a superior language to English; and since in Latin you must not end a sentence with a preposition and cannot split an infinitive (for the Latin infinitive is always a single word), these grave pundits insisted that writers of English should abide by the same rules. But it's far worse to tie your writing in knots trying to avoid a split infinitive than to boldly go ahead and split one.

The Fowler brothers thought the split infinitive 'an ugly thing', but the idea that splitting or not splitting infinitives makes the difference between a good and a bad writer they called a 'curious superstition'. And writers who fancy that such a construction as 'to be really understood' is a split infinitive, which it is not, and mangle their sentences accordingly, putting their adverbs in strange places, incurred H.W. Fowler's contempt. He called them 'deaf to the normal rhythm of English sentences'.

Are apostrophes important? And what are the rules about their use?

It can't be denied that the apostrophe, after a reign of only 200 years or so, is on the way out. It has largely disappeared from shop fascias and is nowadays rarely seen in the High Street except as the so-called 'greengrocer's apostrophe' ('apple's 40p. a pound'). One job the apostrophe properly does is to stand in for a missing letter; but in that role it often gets confused with the sign known as the 'open single quotation mark'. Thus a well-known cereal firm prints 'Fruit 'n Fibre' on its packets instead of 'Fruit 'n Fibre'—which strictly speaking should be 'Fruit 'n' Fibre', since the last letter of 'and' is missing as well as the first.

For the time being—i.e. for as long as there is a consensus that printed English requires their correct use—the incorrect use of apostrophes in print looks careless and should be avoided. Most English words, singular or plural, that end in a letter other than *s* form the possessive by adding *'s*; here the apostrophe always comes before the added *s* (child's play, children's playground). Singular nouns that end in *s* usually form the possessive by adding *'s* (ass's milk), but where the added *s* would not be pronounced it is normally omitted and an apostrophe alone is used (for goodness' sake, for conscience' sake). Plural nouns that end in *s* form the possessive by adding an apostrophe, which here always comes after the *s* (boys' shoes). Modern names and surnames ending in *s* generally add *'s* in the possessive (St James's Park), but ancient names ending in *s* generally don't (Jesus' words). Abbreviations follow the rule, adding *'s* in the singular (an MP's speech or, alternatively, an M.P.'s speech), *s'* in the plural (MPs' votes or M.P.s' votes); the plural of an abbreviation needs no apostrophe (MPs or M.P.s, not MP's or M.P.'s; the 1990s, not the 1990's). Nor is there any apostrophe in hers, ours, theirs, yours, and its (this last is a possessive pronoun and adjective; 'it's', where the apostrophe is obligatory, is a contraction of 'it is').

You say nothing about preferring the active voice to the passive. Is this important?

A lot of needless fuss is made about this. At first glance 'George took the dog for a walk' is clearer and more direct than 'the dog was taken for a walk by George'; but there are contexts in which, for the sake of emphasis or contrast or euphony, the passive version would be stronger and more appropriate. It hardly seems so in the following example, however: 'Four months later, a 90th birthday party was thrown for him by his daughter' (Dea Birkett). This suggests that someone other than his daughter had at first thought of giving the party. Better: 'Four months later his daughter threw a 90th-birthday party for him'.

There is no doubt that *excessive* use of the passive voice soon becomes tiresome. It is certainly so on Radio 4 news programmes, where almost every item seems to start with a passive: the government never announces anything; everything *is announced by* the government. But many grammar checkers on word processors seem obsessed with tracking down the passive voice, so that virtually every sentence containing 'is' or 'was' is exasperatingly queried. Rest assured that if most of your verbs are in the active voice few readers will ever notice your occasional use of the passive. Here, as elsewhere, you shouldn't tie your hands with 'rules' that no English writer of repute has ever given a toss about.

How do I get started as a writer?

There are countless ways of answering this question. Often those who ask it have another question at the back of their mind: 'What do I write about?' This needs answering first. And the most helpful answer, for the beginner, is two-pronged: 'Write about what *you know*, and write about what *you're really interested in.*' With a little thought, whoever has the tiniest spark of ambition to be a writer can find ample material in their own life, work, and hobbies, and in those of family, friends, and workmates.

Imaginative writing lies outside the scope of this booklet. But the same answer broadly applies to the short-story writer, the novelist, the dramatist, and the poet. The use that aspirant creative writers ultimately make of the material thus to hand may of course be very different from what the would-be journalist or essayist does with it. But no one, however modest their aim, can hope to interest others in what they write unless they write knowledgeably and out of deep interest and commitment. Otherwise their writing comes over as flat and stale. 'Nothing worthwhile is done without passion', said a great philosopher; and of no human activity is this truer than of writing.

But if you must cut your coat according to your cloth you must also, if you hope to sell the coat you've made, have some regard to fashion. This means, for the writer, studying the market. To send an article on some aspect of yachting to a magazine that caters for golfers or computer buffs would be folly. The *Writer's and Artist's Yearbook*, a reference book that should be readily accessible in your local library, provides essential information on magazines' and publishers' requirements. Study it. Then study several back issues of whatever publication strikes you as suitable. This will give you guidance on such matters as style and length.

Lastly, don't let initial rejection discourage you. Comparatively few writers have ever succeeded at their first attempt. Most professional writers spend years learning their trade, and for many those are years of frequent disappointment and frustration. For every ounce of talent and passion you have, you need a ton of perseverance.

How do I get information?
It's a good idea to keep your own files of cuttings from newspapers and magazines on subjects that interest you, and you would do well to make this task an invariable daily habit. You should jot down on each cutting the name and publication date of the newspaper or magazine you've taken it from. Time spent organising your cuttings into clearly labelled folders or large envelopes is never wasted. It's a mistake to let your files grow too bulky; every so often you should winnow them, discarding whatever cuttings you are unlikely to need again.

After your own files, your local library should be your next port of call. The librarian is trained to point inquirers in the right direction by suggesting appropriate reference books, which include bibliographies, annual indexes to *The Times* and to periodicals, and various other guides.

When you need further, more specialised, help you should ask for it from those who know more than you. Most large firms, and many local councils and other organisations, have a public relations officer or press officer, whose job includes providing information to people who telephone or write in. Most authors are glad to answer questions from readers of their books, especially if a letter is accompanied by the courtesy of a stamped addressed envelope. Send your letter to the author's publishers and they will forward it.

Can you recommend any books for further reading, apart from the works of reference mentioned in Chapter 1?
The most useful book of its kind is Sir Ernest Gowers, *The Complete Plain Words*, edited by Sidney Greenbaum and Janet Whitcut (1986). First published in 1954, this was intended mainly for civil servants whose task is to write letters to the rest of us, and it has done much to hold back the sludge-tide of officialese over the past third of a century. It is packed with sensible advice.

An older book from which much can still be learnt is Robert Graves and Alan Hodge, *The Reader over your Shoulder: A Handbook for Writers of English Prose* (1943). Long out of print, this can still be found in some second-hand bookshops and local libraries. It subjects passages from writers well known in the 1930s and 1940s to detailed and often scalding analysis and rewriting.

INDEX